EATING
Her Wedding Dress

The Ragged Sky Poetry Series

Susquehanna and *The Confidence Man* by Michael R. Brown

The Luxury of Obstacles by Elizabeth Danson

Loose Parlance by Daniel A. Harris

Little Knitted Sister by Ellen Foos

Dog Watch by Valerie Lawson

Moonmilk and Other Poems by Carlos Hernández Peña

Between Silence and Praise by Elizabeth Anne Socolow

Penguins in a Warming World by Anca Vlasopolos

Escape Velocity by Arlene Weiner

EATING
Her Wedding Dress

A Collection of Clothing Poems

Edited by Vasiliki Katsarou,
Ruth O'Toole,
and Ellen Foos

Ragged Sky Press
Princeton, New Jersey

Published by Ragged Sky Press
PO Box 312
Annandale, NJ 08801

Library of Congress Cataloging-in-Publication Data

Eating her wedding dress : a collection of clothing poems/edited by Vasiliki Katsarou,
Ruth O'Toole, and Ellen Foos.—1st ed.
    p. cm.
ISBN 978-1-933974-06-4 (pbk. : alk. paper)
1. Clothing and dress—Poetry. I. Katsarou, Vasiliki. II. O'Toole, Ruth. III.
Foos, Ellen, 1955-
PN6110.C59E37 2009
808.81'93559—dc22   2008052541

A list of acknowledgments appears in the back of this book.

This book is composed in Garamond Pro and Futura Book.

Interior design by Patti Capaldi

raggedsky.com

Manufactured in the United States of America

First Edition

CONTENTS

Alteration

Selvage

Sheer

In art, a dress is never just a dress; nor in life either.
—Mason Cooley

As the daughter of a seamstress, I have always been struck by the intense hand-labor of sewing, by the deft movement of nimble fingers, so different from the act of writing. My mother grew up in a small Greek village with no local secondary school, and daughters of her generation were not sent away for a high school education. So my mother's parents apprenticed her to a local seamstress. She excelled almost immediately, and her talent, diligence, and business acumen would provide her five-member family with its sole source of wartime income.

One of the stories my mother wove into legend for her children was of a three-day sojourn into the mountains, ascending to sew a wedding dress for the gypsies. They were itinerant shepherd families who still live today in the hinterlands of modern Greece. In exchange for the hand-sewn, all-white dress with a pleated bodice and full skirt, my mother described how she was paid in kind—with cheese, white *flokati* rugs, and thick woven blankets crafted in geometric patterns called "*velentzes*."

Meanwhile, back at home, my mother's elder sister was busy embroidering both her own dowry and my mother's: pillowcases stitched with garlands of flowers and initials, cloths embroidered with the colorful patterns of Greek folk art. As she sent potential suitors away, my aunt continued to weave, crochet, and embroider, her hands never idle—a veritable Penelope.

My mother's entrepreneurial ambitions were cut short when she was married to my father and emigrated to the small New England town where I was born. She spoke no English and couldn't drive, but she did have a sewing machine, and in her spare moments she crafted exquisite red velvet dresses for me, blue velveteen knickers for my younger brother and, at my request, a whole wardrobe of miniature doll clothing. But woven into the fabric my mother sewed for me were her own unspoken desires.

The poems collected here, like my childhood experience, reveal the rich language of clothing—from Barbie clothes and evening wear, to socks, mittens, ties, diapers, and even body bags. Poets from far and wide have responded poignantly and with humor to our call for poetry about clothing. There is no denying the powerful effect of the closet on memory and imagination.

There are poems about clothing as identity—which can be altered, loosened, unloosed, or unleashed. There are poems about clothing as a consumer item, and about clothing styles as objects of desire that can never be attained. Clothing also serves as memento, and as metaphor for the body itself, as a second skin.

Clothes not only "make the man," as Twain famously declared, but they also make us: brides and grooms, shoppers, mourners, flappers, and penitents. Clothes mark and transform us just as much as we transform them. And as we undergo this transformation, clothes sometimes seem to displace us, as Lynn Wagner suggests in her poem, "The Little Black Dress:"

> The little black dress goes to cocktail parties—
> orders something with milk in it, *like maybe*
> *a White Russian.* The little black dress titters
> and flirts

Given the matriarchal history of weaving and sewing, and the vast array of choices for women's wear in Western culture, it is perhaps not surprising that most of the poets in this volume are women, and one of the threads (so to speak) that runs through their poems is the relationship between women and their mothers and grandmothers through both presentation (dressing up) and alteration (sewing, mending, transfiguring). One powerful nostalgic glance is taken at the changing fashions of a mother in Celia Lisset Alvarez's "1969":

> The gingham
> and the silk. The woolen skirts
> you'd wear in winter, the cardigans
> with round pearl buttons. I can smell
>
> Your lavender face powder, if I try
> although who would dare to touch you.

It might seem as if male poets have less opportunity for expression through the text and texture of their body's covering. Yet, it is this very ambivalence that is so poignantly noted in a poem like James Richardson's "The Family of Ties":

When each disguise is abandoned as hopeless,
they are the weight around our necks. Their minds,
narrow or broad, their careers, checkered
or solid, were ours, and we are dismayed

to find that they always fit.

As textile archaeologist Elizabeth Wayland Barber points out in her fascinating book, *Women's Work, the First 20,000 Years: Women, Cloth and Society in Early Times* (W.W. Norton & Co., 1994):

> Clothing, right from our first direct evidence twenty thousand years ago, has been the handiest solution to conveying social messages, visually, silently, continuously.

The wedding dress is the iconic example of clothing bearing a message. Like a gift in an exquisite wrapper, the wedding dress presents the bride to her groom and to the community as a whole. In its artistry—the exquisite beading or lace or line—the wedding dress expresses the great symbolic value of this event in our culture. The collection's title poem, Eileen Malone's "Eating Her Wedding Dress," is a unique take on this most storied of garments:

> once again, I the old and unmarried
> press my face to the wedding feast
> eat pearls of pickled onions
> raw oysters in tiny ivory shells

The poet takes hold of this charged symbol, literally and metaphorically—tasting it and transforming it in an utterly new way.

Clothes can also seem to take on our own mortality. In their persistent materiality, old clothes appear to us like the ghosts of past selves. We part with loved clothes unwillingly or sometimes we inhabit clothes in order to reanimate them, as in Christine Gelineau's mysterious "Inheritance":

> I
> am the
> woman they give
> dead women's
> clothes to
> I live easily
> in them . . .

This anthology is arranged into four parts: First is *Presentation*, which includes poems of self-presentation and identity, and about how deep a superficial layer can be. The second section is *Alteration*, concerned with the transformation of clothing through personal history, and how what we wear changes us. *Selvage* refers to the visible seams, the construction, the underside of the handicraft of sewing—and poetry. Finally, *Sheer* encompasses the talismanic or magical quality of clothing—which Barber credits with the ability "to preserve fertility, encourage prosperity, offer protection, or even to curse."

In her poem "To Clotho, in care of Sears," Jean Hollander invokes one of the divine spinners of fate in Greek myth: "Dear Clotho, long ago I got/a faulty pattern and bad goods." If, as the ancient Greeks believed, one's lifespan is a thread, then our choices in life, and all our creations, poetic or otherwise, are the weavings we undertake with our free will.

The seam, the pleat, the line—the architecture of clothing—is an inspiration and a metaphor for the poetic line, and for the craft of poetry. Ultimately, skin itself may be thought of as a similar kind of provisional covering, one that can never be left behind in this life. Bobbi Lurie's "January Sales" appears to be a poem about shopping, but takes a turn in its final lines:

> And not until I lie naked in my bed
> can I feel
>
> the white longing in my bones
> which can not be dressed.

We hope you will enjoy this book of poems about clothing, in all its textures and patterns, the veils and unveilings, the shifts and the slips.

Vasiliki Katsarou
Annandale, New Jersey

Presentation

Well, you look so pretty in it
Honey, can I jump on it sometime?

—Bob Dylan, "Leopard-Skin Pill-Box Hat"

Apparel

Stop me if I've told you
   this
    before

the way I've
   worn a garden snake
    as arch support
     under my bare foot,
      for just a moment,
an unplanned fitting for
   both of us

a hummingbird
  as a raucous earring
    for a golden flash
    of a second

kingfishers, grackles, and bats
   as potential hair combs

the tight beauty mark of a leech
   in a sweet summer swimming hole

mosquitoes, of course,
   as ruby body paint

fluid mutable ant tattoos

and the gift of a
   shimmering dragonfly brooch
   on a bare and
    blushing shoulder

LORRAINE HENRIE LINS

Barbie Image

She sits in a heap of pink shimmer and taffeta—
plastic arms and hips, breasts and legs;
humming a tune she, alone, knows.
I watch as she tips her head
left to right, the way an idea finds
a sculpture in the clay.
She plucks a blonde by the
ankles and begins jamming her
feet-first into a crispy, white strapless
wedding gown, twisting thighs and ass,
belly and boob deep into Velcro seams.
She wrestles rubber ankles and legs into
Ken's On-the-Town black loafers
and manipulates his red, Lifeguard-Ken jacket
over her wineglass-grip hands.
The once flawless glow of blonde tresses,
now cut to a marine-regulation trim,
gets a wet-fingered press and with a straight-armed
gesture, she juts the doll toward me,
telling me Barbie's beautiful now and ready
to go to the Acme. The idea of Barbie used
to frighten my concept of mothering,
threaten the self-confined mold
I wanted her to grow within,
but seeing her bending the ultimate woman to her will,
fitting it with her idea of beauty,
makes me wonder why more women don't
sit to play with Barbie.

My Daughter's Pajamas

In my dream the neighbor girl and her father
are night prowling through the dark trees of our yard
looking for Barbie's bathrobe.

It is black and white, maybe fur, they say
moving through the bushes. It seems a forest
has grown around the house.

The girl's small hand grips the hard breasts and long legs
of the doll clad in thin pajamas. The father has both hands
thrust in his pockets.

They have looked everywhere and I am worried
it is so dark I can't see them and do not understand
how they lost it.

Then my daughter comes outside
still damp from her shower, I turn and see her hair,
a mass of dark gold tangles,

her narrow hairless body, round breast buds exposed
as she dries her back with a towel
and calls to the neighbors,

We'll find it, don't worry! and goes on drying herself
unaware of being naked, unashamed of this body
which is all she has ever slept in.

MARCIA ALDRICH

White Blouse

White blouse (hwit blaus) n. 1. A long loose over
garment that resembles a shirt or smock in the color
of new snow or milk. See: *uniforms of perfection.*
First worn by Deborah in the sixth grade
at Jefferson Elementary. Starched cotton, did not cling
or collect electricity. Most importantly it did not shine.
New, crisp, unwrinkled, unblemished, blank. *Side note*:
stains set quickly, the white blouse must be immersed
immediately in cold water. Even then, stains
may not come out. The white blouse
must be ironed, must have a shape.
Deborah's mother washed and ironed
her white blouse, maintained its pristine shape.
Warning: When Deborah returned from her
suicide attempt, the bandages wrapped
about her wrists matched her white blouse.
Her mother believed that Deborah
would be safe inside the white blouse.
She was not.
2. A loose fitting garment esp. for women
that covers the body from the neck
to the waist, free from spot or blemish, marked
by uprightness and purity. *History*: born
from women in uniforms of virtue—brides,
waitresses, nurses, nuns, cheery mothers
on milk cartons, on billboards, bakers of bread.
Caretakers of the body, caretakers of the soul.
See: Wilkie Collins' *The Woman in White*, Emily Dickinson,
The Belle of Amherst. Unflappable in the midst
of breakdown, catastrophe. In the white blouse,
these women can nurse anything. But when

the woman removes her white blouse,
she collapses. The white blouse held
her together in uprightness. Without the white blouse
her body pours forth. 3. Because the white blouse
has assumed such a formidable presence over time,
the two words, white and blouse,
have formed a new unit, *whiteblouse*
which hangs in the heavens,
beyond pain, beyond death.

JILL STEIN

Lace, 1963

Walking down Flatbush at three o'clock
every store window called to us
to join the throng of the most beautiful.
But it was the lace suits that won our hearts—
like paper doilies, snowflakes
splayed on silk,
the buttons, small lace candies,
each of us bride and businesswoman
wrapped in one.
When we entered the closet of mirrors
we swooned at our reflection.
We were glorious from every angle—
twin debutantes
ready to step out into the bright glare of day
and ride our bus home triumphantly.
Afterwards, we didn't understand how it had happened.
We were like amnesiacs
or fickle lovers lying to ourselves about the past.
When we took the dresses back
we didn't speak.

Chapeaux

My daughter reaches deep into another trunk
and pulls out hats, gasping with laughter
as she discovers cloche and cartwheel,
pillbox, tam, beret and toque,
all of them crumbling, dropping crumbs
of felt and feather on the dusty floor.

I take one from her hands and put it on,
pull the elastic band (how young and supple it still feels!)
under my hair, peer through the crumpled veil.

Paris once meant hats, romance—
how could I honeymoon among those windows
full of chic *chapeaux,* without trying them on?
And his eyes were mirrors brighter than any
I'd ever looked in, telling me I was beautiful

in feathers, beige and white, that curled
around my face, crushed velvet, gold as honey,
that wide-brimmed straw with orange poppies,
in hats like wheels, dizzy flat discs, in pearls,
felt flowers, plumes, and veils to flirt through—
Mlle. Lili murmuring *Parfait, madame, parfait,*

as I swam in delirium, at all that beauty,
at being named *madame* at last, at crossing bridges
through bright clouds of love, and all the future
opening in long uncluttered boulevards
and rising, airy, solid, like the Tour Eiffel.

JORIE GRAHAM

San Sepolcro

In this blue light
    I can take you there,
snow having made me
    a world of bone
seen through to. This
    is my house,

my section of Etruscan
    wall, my neighbor's
lemontrees, and, just below
    the lower church,
the airplane factory.
    A rooster

crows all day from mist
    outside the walls.
There's milk on the air,
    ice on the oily
lemonskins. How clean
    the mind is,

holy grave. It is this girl
    by Piero
della Francesca, unbuttoning
    her blue dress,
her mantle of weather,
    to go into

labor. Come, we can go in.
    It is before
the birth of god. No-one
    has risen yet

to the museums, to the assembly
line—bodies

and wings—to the open air
market. This is
what the living do: go in.
It's a long way.
And the dress keeps opening
from eternity

to privacy, quickening.
Inside, at the heart,
is tragedy, the present moment
forever stillborn,
but going in, each breath
is a button

coming undone, something terribly
nimble-fingered
finding all of the stops.

My Bra

My bra, it keeps my breasts in equilibrium.
It stops them lolling,
makes them conform.

My bra, it makes my breasts be fair,
molded to hide flaws, absence,
age and arousal.

My bra, it makes my breasts concealed things,
thus objects to adore.

Underneath, my heart,
a hideous, unbridled growth,
peers out, ticking.

BOBBI LURIE

January Sales

It's the January sales
and I'm buying.

Trapped in the endless, airless halls,
nullified through the phosphorescent fluorescence

and the lonely beating of my thoughts,
walking behind all the girlfriends,

as I lug my bags, sorry already
for the weight of fashion.

And when I get home
I see other clothes hanging

hanging in my closet...
new, unused, reflecting all the places

I did not go,
the ways I was not seen.

And not until I lie naked in my bed
can I feel

the white longing in my bones
which can not be dressed.

HOWARD LIEBERMAN

Mall Store

This one
is the epitome,
contains
3 thousand, three hundred and thirty-five
stylized creations,
all practically the same
but subtly
differentiated
in color. O,
tell me how to breathe.
Tell me how to think.
I'd better wait outside.

DIANE ELAYNE DEES

The New Recruits

The big box near my house sells
pink camo togs for little girls.
In my dark visions,
pre-teens slog through the desert
in Little Mermaid combat boots,
carrying Hello Kitty walkie-talkies.
Preening like Jessica and Britney,
they load their M-16s
and toss their shiny hair.
When their jeep is attacked,
they scream like they did
when their mothers took them
to see Matchbox Twenty
and let them buy official concert Ts.
Soon they are covered with sand,
their screams muffled by blasts,
until a glittery white phosphorescence
is all that remains of them.

If Paris Hilton Wrote Poetry

Shoes.
Shoes.
Cute.
Shoes.
Me.
Cute shoes.

Shoes. Shoes.
Me. Me.
Cute.
Cute.
Me.

ELLEN FOOS

Vestments

The priests take the cake,
our hosanna high warriors—
glorified and insular
in liturgical purple.
Stoles wrapped over shoulders,
with two hands they raise a cup,
kneel in showy surrender—
trousers peeping out under robes.
I throw them my quarters.

And the black-clad nuns,
our so-be-it foot soldiers
in clumsy shoes, stiff bibs,
chained by a rosary-bead belt—
nothing to suggest undergarments.
Dark horsemen, chalk-powdered hands,
no nonsense in the pews
as they pass by.
I toss them my homework.

DANIEL A. HARRIS

Attire

Sometimes, making a *shiva* call
or at a funeral, you have seen them,
an elderly couple mourning
their eldest or perhaps middle child,
glancing a little warily
at the odd thing the other wears
on blouse or lapel (you can tell
how much effort it's taken them
to put on clothes today, their hearts
being undressed)—that little extra
piece of clothing, the thin black ribbon
of customary bombazine,
a tatter neatly cut, their badge
of ruin flashing as if it were
the only stitch they wore.

CHARLES SIMIC

My Shoes

Shoes, secret face of my inner life:
Two gaping toothless mouths,
Two partly decomposed animal skins
Smelling of mice-nests.

My brother and sister who died at birth
Continuing their existence in you,
Guiding my life
Toward their incomprehensible innocence.

What use are books to me
When in you it is possible to read
The Gospel of my life on earth
And still beyond, of things to come?

I want to proclaim the religion
I have devised for your perfect humility
And the strange church I am building
With you as the altar.

Ascetic and maternal, you endure:
Kin to oxen, to Saints, to condemned men,
With your mute patience, forming
The only true likeness of myself.

HARVEY STEINBERG

Morning Psalm of Sox

A seismograph
my sox rumble on
not rustle
wrenched from nether world
untorn
unfrayed
relinquished to a tumbling
drum
wetted
scoured
and dried
whole for
wholesome
freshened days

methodist makeover

the huge pile of clothes donated to our church
rummage sale by the war widow her departed
husband a young man just forty-four his taste
ran fairly medium along with his size 34 × 32
trousers brown blue tan gray and black dockers
16 ½ × 34 button down shirts and knit pullovers
to keep the wives away from the pile of clothes
my size the rumor emerges these clothes were
salvaged from state funeral homes taken off
dead men after their viewing everyone knows
the body is always buried naked all my size I
won't try on a single piece of my new wardrobe

WALLY GLICKMAN

Makinglove

The night is cold,
the way is far,
I reach for you
and there you are.
Can't you see you'll always be...my glove.

Ah your skin,
that little rip,
the feel within
each fingertip.
Oh you must know I need you so...my glove.

So bring on stormy weather,
let it freeze forever,
you know I'm into leather,
whenever we're together.

It seems we each
had lost a mate,
we're both alone,
so tempting fate
I picked you up
there on the street.
Our fingers touched,
it felt so sweet,
I put you on,
my knees grew weak.
The way you clung!
No need to speak,
it was profound. I knew I'd found...my glove.

A sonnet could be written
on your fur—soft as a kitten.
I've never been so smitten
by any muff or mitten.

The night is long,
the way is far.
I know it's wrong—
and so bizarre
it should be banned—
and yet...and yet it feels so grand
walking with you hand in hand.
Oh can't you see you'll always be...my glove.

To hell with fame or riches.
Even when it itches
you've got something which is
keeping me in stitches.

Oh my dear you give me fits
and though it's true you have no tits,
you make it up with five big clits...
and that hand job at the Ritz!
Remember darling what we did?
Kidding, kidding. Oh you kid!
Even when all breath is gone,
I'll never cease to put you on,
my sacred sin, my second skin...my glove.

ELIZABETH ANNE SOCOLOW

A Gift of Mittens after Many Years Alone Wearing Gloves

Am I really thankful for this gift that makes
these fellows, my fingers, nestle
near each other naked
in the cold?
A litter of four thrown together in one sack
so intimate, the heat next to heat
they generate.
I blush at such familiarity, such
sleep after this many years alone
in gloves, in bed.

JAMES RICHARDSON

The Family of Ties

When, after their fashion, the jackets,
shirts and trousers fold up, or cling
to the lean past, or embarrass themselves
out of existence, the ties still hang around.

Listening at the backs of doors, frozen
against the walls of closets, they can
never be disowned. We seem to know
that it is useless to try to forget.

When each disguise is abandoned as hopeless,
they are the weight around our necks. Their minds,
narrow or broad, their careers, checkered
or solid, were ours, and we are dismayed

to find that they always fit. Just when we thought
we had changed, there they are, signposts of rigidity,
racks of humiliations:
the motley, waiting for each new man.

DONNA VORREYER

What Not to Wear

Rejection is plaid.
The threads of loss
and humiliation cross
from side to side, each
its own color, woven
over and under like
excuses, like lies, ugly
and unbecoming on
everyone, only suited
for the linings of rain
coats so no one can
see the chaos under
the cover of dark.

Showing Thong

The whole cliché—
the platinum blonde
melted into her oh so obvious
"drinking team" tee shirt,
in her peep-toe shoes sauntering
clickity through the cheap seats;
the smile, the nod, the implied
apology for the little sister
on the third base side
trying to catch a foul.

SHOSHAUNA SHY

What Shall I Wear to Meet Your Wife

since we want to convince her
my presence in your life
is harmless?
Not the skirt with the wide waistband
that made my sister-in-law gasp
You fit into that after three kids - !
Not the *take-no-shit* Durangos
I wear line-dancing in mountain towns,
nor the angora sweater that induces
all and sundry to rub up against me.
I won't wear the spinster cardigan
with its embroidered blossoms
she'll know for a ruse
or the Lee Riders that make my rear end
look cupcake-cute.
No, let me don the diamond
my husband gave me when
we had money to burn;
the *no-lie-I'm-flat-as-a-washboard*
sweater; the velvet headband
reminiscent of every Plain Jane
grade eight all boys ignored,
and whom she herself pitied.

IRENE WILLIS

The Yellow Shirt

Every day in his house
he likes what his eye
falls on:
his blue bathrobe
worn in the seat
his slippers
with the soft suede soles
and suede tops
the brown leather chair
the dent in the ottoman
where he rests
the same heel every evening
one leg crossed
over the other, his bottom foot
digging in, the way he likes it
the remote control at his elbow
the small dog
asleep across his knees.
He likes her eyebrows
her beard
the black lashes under her brows
and her eyes, like the agates
he shot as a kid
on the hill near the high school.
He likes his wife
in her soft old blue jersey slacks
and yellow shirt
the mailman coming up to the porch
dropping letters and bills
through the slot in the door.
He likes greeting the dog
walking the dog

feeding the dog
putting the dog to bed.
He likes turning off the TV
and going upstairs to bed himself.
And his wife can see him
liking all of this
from the faint smile on his face
as he goes about his business
of liking the house, his dog
his wife, the remote control.
And she likes his liking it
and he can feel her
liking him liking it.
This is a state
that some will recognize
and call love
and that others will think
is either less or more
than they are entitled to
and so will consider divorce,
break-up, suicide, murder,
taking a lover.
Meanwhile, of course,
the man in the blue bathrobe
and his wife in the yellow shirt
go on as before. The man
carries a picture of the dog
in his wallet on trips
and sets it up on the dresser
before turning out the light.
His wife
sends the yellow shirt
to the cleaner's
and it comes back

with broken buttons
a shoulder pad hanging by a thread
and a tag hooked to a button saying
Sorry. We tried and tried
but couldn't remove this stain.
It's about this time
she begins to think
something has gone out
of their marriage.
So she tells him
about how it used to be
and how it is now
and he says
Whatever happened
to that yellow shirt you used to wear?

Alteration

Life is the garment we continually alter,
but which never seems to fit.

—David McCord

CELIA LISSET ALVAREZ

1969

How kerchiefed you saw yourself,
riding in your fishers, the convertible
a big blue whale you'd filleted into
a rowboat, your shirt of picnic colors

A mother-flag, a summer. Those Jackie-O
glasses rested on your impossible
cheekbones, pink as Barbie's. Your
brown arms and the single freckle

On your neck, well. The gingham
and the silk. The woolen skirts
you'd wear in winter, the cardigans
with round pearl buttons. I can smell

Your lavender face powder, if I try
although who would dare to touch you.
Even your aprons were starched and
trimmed in scratchy lace.

Those square-heeled pumps you wore
made all the rooms so tidy. Your silver
vacuum exhaled all the promises of tomorrow,
those General Electric years.

Tonight, meatloaf and dehydrated potatoes.
In a few more years, the cocktails will run dry,
and your collars will be pointed into spears.
Your static hose will cling to your polyester

Dress, and you'll flip your bob around
like a hedgehog. Trade in the convertible
for a Monte Carlo, paint your nails.
Untouchable still.

SHERRILL ALESIAK

Hanging Clothes

Mondays, my mother would heave
the creaking wicker basket
up the basement stairs
to the clotheslines outside,
wipe them clean,
then with wooden clothespins,
hang sheets—corners connecting—
my dad's factory hankies, pillowcases, and shirts,
fastidiously pinning underpants on the inside line
to shy away from neighbors.

Clothes hung.
Years flap by, nearly ready
to take down and gather in a basket.
A load accomplished.
It all comes out in the wash—almost all—
except for the awkward haul of Alzheimer's
she carries inside her cinderblock room
with the slim locker
that chokes her labeled clothes,
no longer able to breathe in the heat of the day.

From lawn chairs on the deck,
my t-shirts crisp
in the dry mouth of the wind
to stand straight as a movie screen
when I pull my childhood over my head
and, momentarily blindfolded,
glimpse spirits,
clothed in sheets and shirts,
fluttering and dancing
to the rhythm of the wind.

JANET BARRY

Goodwill

A shoe,
which last I wore
in a field full
of milkweed,
clover, vetch,
summer blooms
I loved too much,
and lay in too long.

And a silk scarf,
blown off one day
across the pond,
brief flight
above gathered geese,
then caught
among the reeds,
withered, the way
an old newspaper
turns sodden
against the gutter.

And how long
since I've worn
this shabby sweater?
Fall colors padded
against the chill,
cuffs rubbed raw
to the color
of old leaves,
spent firewood.

It is that chill
I would have protected
you from,
my love,

protected me from,
a coat, without its zipper,
a hat turned shapeless,
a boot, missing
its sole.

And these gloves,
work worn,
leather fingers
buffed to nothingness,
stitching unraveled,
each slice and stain
a rock cairn
anchoring a fogbound
mountain.

I brushed the dog,
my love,
with these gloves.
Tugged weeds,
culled sumac,
choke-cherry,
pruned the roses.
I hung a tire-swing
from the copper beech
in the backyard.

Yes, take
these gloves.
I set them down
just the other day
in a field full of milkweed,
stalks browning under
autumn blue,
vetch, clutching
at the roots.

CAROLYN A. DAHL

Cutting Cloth for Rag Rugs

Dresses bloom like summer zinnias
    in the rummage-sale clothes my grandmother presses to her chest.
I sit at her feet, still child-blonde, holding tiny scissors
    to cut clothes to rags for handwoven rugs.

Grandmother lifts the bundle above her head,
    lets the clothes fall slowly
One-by-one the colors land: blue skirt, yellow dress,
    red blouse. A purple scarf she catches in mid-air.

She calls me *Stina* in Swedish.
    I hope the name means love, like how she pulls
A man's shirt toward her by its arms,
    or finds sugar lumps in apron pockets, inviting me
To dip sweet snowballs in coffee
    she boils with eggshells for clarity and color.

We sit on last year's woven rugs, her flashing blades
    snip open a coat's underarm seam.
With practiced hand, she flattens the cloth,
    cuts it into strips, winds its former life into a tight ball.
I pull a pretty dress from the pile by its hem,
    Lay it before me like Christmas, red taffeta,
Gold buttons, a metal-toothed zipper
    smiling on its way down the spine.

I cover my body with the dress,
    compare waists to measure how far I've yet to grow
To become what I imagine a woman is.
    I want to try on lives, slip my skinny identity into
The folds of a woman's party dress,
    heady with spicy perfume.
I hope my grandmother won't mind, if today
    I don't cut apart the woman I want to become.

ANCA VLASOPOLOS

Loosed Garments

how the seams now stretch
in clothes that used to hang loosely
zippers become perverse
and buttons move just out of reach of loop

as you rummage ever more frantically
inside the closet
where your sight picks out less and less
you bend to gather up
an old silk shirt
and make out
shining
like polished silver
in the right corner
an outfit you'd forgotten
in the left corner
another you've never noticed
sending sparks
bunched up

skins
as the scientists
and hunters and collectors
are fond of calling them

look
this one fits
so well
like
well
like skin
with such a largesse of paw

your girth now seems
positively svelte
muscled
ready for
a swim in Arctic waters
a sweet meal
of seal

the other dazzles
like shooting stars
bejeweled velvet
breezes incarnate
this one will cling
and whisper
caress
and give you
what nothing
in this overcrowded closet
of your past shapes
can offer
—wings

BEATRICE M. HOGG

Fabulous

(In memory of Richard H. Person, 1/03/41–9/19/94)

It has been almost fourteen years,
But just a whiff
Of Paco Rabanne—
Brings you back to me.

I can see you standing there
Navy blue designer pinstripe suit
Italian leather shoes, discreet socks
Red silk around your neck
And peeking from your breast pocket—
Expensive but understated jewelry,
Every hair in place—
From Afro to moustache.

You were fabulous—
How I loved you—
African caftans—
Jumpsuits—
US Air Force full dress uniform—
You knew no fear...

If heaven has a dress code—
You are behind the Velvet Rope—
Right next to God.

ELAINE EQUI

Armani Weather

In that long
navy blue
cashmere coat,
he was made
to do nothing
but lean against
tall buildings.
A somber
exclamation point,
eating an apple—
turning it slowly
into ballet.
How extravagant
yet restrained,
the way he wears
the space
around his body
loosely.
Even the light matches,
pale and cold
and slightly green,
like the apple
against his dark skin.

ENRIQUETA CARRINGTON

Suite of Shoes

I.

In my true childhood, shoes always came in pairs,
of which we each had two, Good and Everyday.
But a shoe has a life cycle as it wears;
new Good Ones, much to my father's dismay,

would become necessary, and since they
were a half-inch larger, ah, the pride they gave!
Then the old Good Ones became the shoes for play,
while old Everydays would step into their grave.

Because this was a rule with my mother:
clothes we might get from cousins, second-hand,
and then pass on from brother to brother
to sister, as long as the threads would withstand,

but not deformed shoes—those she made sure
were never handed down, even to the poor.

II.

The shoes of orphanhood trudged in
next.
All order shattered,
we stumbled over smithereens.

Our steps mincing,
feet bound in too-small
prisons,
we limped, until we cut holes
to accommodate
growing
toes.

In old photos
I see the peeping
socks,
feet longer than the leather soles
that snarled
to show their
tacks.

The desolation of those years is there
in the footwear
as much as in over-sized
eyes and bony
necks.

One brother had two shoes
but not a
pair.

III.

Now we remove them when we enter our home,
and pair upon pair, male, female, large, small,
return from the many places they roam

to hold their gossipy gatherings in our hall
while, by their side, the little shoes gambol,
huaraches, pumps, moccasins, galoshes sprawl

discussing the best path for a ramble,
the friendly disputes of boots rising above
sneaker speakers' cracks at sandal scandal.

Each shoe is imprinted with the cadence of
the run, the purposeful walk, the calm stroll,
the joyful leaps of someone I love—

a shoe has at least the ghost of a soul,
personal as a voice or the mark of a pen;
so Vincent painted his spirit in a sole.

All these pairs I round up now and then,
send them firmly upstairs, but the group proceeds
to gather yet again, and I say amen,

as if this house of ours were inhabited
by a family of happy centipedes.

PAUL MULDOON

The Treaty

My grandfather Frank Regan, cross-shanked, his shoulders in a moult,
steadies the buff
of his underparts against the ledge of the chimney bluff
of the mud-walled house in Cullenramer

in which, earlier, he had broken open a bolt
of the sky-stuff
and held it to the failing light, having himself failed to balance
   Gormley's cuffs.
"This Collins," Gormley had wagged, "is a right flimflammer."

Cross-shanked against the chimney bluff, he's sizing up what follows
from our being on the verge
of nation-

hood when another broad-lapelled, swallow-tailed swallow
comes at a clip through the dusk-blue serge
to make some last-minute alterations.

MAXINE SUSMAN

Packing for College

A week before you leave
we're in the bedroom sorting clothes.
Three piles: to take, to toss, to leave at home.
Part of me says I'll do your clothes
forever if you'll stay with us. Part says
here's your own jug of detergent,
don't forget to read the labels.
Part says take the other sweatshirt,
it will come in handy, part says
leave it for me to wear around the house
when I miss you. Some things
in your toss pile I regret, but why
should I save what you don't want?
What seemed a closetful of everything
squeezes into one bulging duffel.
I see you there, your quilt on your new bed,
CDs in their rack, posters on the walls,
clothes piled on another floor,
while I sit here in your old room
sorting the come and go between us.

ANDREA POTOS

What I Wore

When my seven-year-old stomps her foot
to keep the Minnie Mouse shirt she wore
her first day of kindergarten,
I don't argue, I can't forget
what lies folded
in my bottom drawer—
the threadbare-at-the-elbow nightgown
strewn with blue and pink roses fading
in the weave, what I wore
that winter night the contractions
came, and we fled the house.
Spots of blood mark the back,
and I never tried to soak them out—
weren't they proof
of the passage that gripped me
those hours
when I crawled across that bridge
over the abyss—my daughter's head
leading the way
to the other side.

MICHAEL R. BROWN

Parents Held Hostage by Hatless Teen

He filled the doorway without threat,
determined to hold his line of want.
With bruised eyes and underslung jaw,
he didn't stand a chance against our unity.
No four-year-old looks softened our heads
as long as his cheeks were discolored,
his puffed lips slow over dogged rhetoric.

Knowing we had been fooled twice
when we discovered the second deception,
knowing our son had put a price
on his head with the hat he'd bought
as soon as he hit town, we drew the line—
no team hats, no starter jackets, no gang colors.

Now, desperate to look like everybody else,
his body filled our doorway,
but we had him right where we wanted him,
stretched out in front of us
instead of lying at the feet of Latin Kings.

JUDITHA DOWD

For the One Who Will Not Be

Last week I passed an expensive shop:
tiny coats swung on a clothesline strung
from front to back in the half-height window.
They were all the same size and navy blue
and piped in red, like the balmacaan
I sewed for my first-born in a winter
that spared nothing but desire.

And tonight I caress your mother's belly,
easing the pain, our loss. Remembering those coats
as they marched away, lighthearted yet resolute.
As if toddlers in a distant room waited
to be buttoned up, their mufflers wound
by someone laughing and patient
who could give them the afternoon.

They hadn't paused for the clumsy prayer
I breathed into their wake.

ARLENE WEINER

Glove Song

I've lost my glove, my good,
my green glove,
that matched my coat so well,
and where will I get another?
Go to the store, there's plenty more.

I've lost my green glove, suede,
that I wore so often, made
part of myself, nights and cold mornings,
and when will I get another?
Be it greener than moss, loss is loss.

I've lost my green suede glove,
dear to me, almost loved,
and who will get me another?
You might have thought, before you bought.

I've lost my dear, my green, my good, my suede glove,
that matched my coat so well, and not less dear
because bought cheap, the last in the store
and out of season,
and how will I do in the cold, in my old coat
with no gloves?
Without a match, you must pinch and patch.

Ah, I've found my dear, my green, my suede glove,
my good, that I treated so badly, dropped
more than once, stepped on,
and now think highly of—
my suede, my dear, my green glove.
Is it so dear, love? Now you've a pair,
take care, take care.
Take more care.

MAXINE KUMIN

How It Is

Shall I say how it is in your clothes?
A month after your death I wear your blue jacket.
The dog at the center of my life recognizes
you've come to visit, he's ecstatic.
In the left pocket, a hole.
In the right, a parking ticket
delivered up last August on Bay State Road.
In my heart, a scatter like milkweed,
a flinging from the pods of the soul.
My skin presses your old outline.
It is hot and dry inside.

I think of the last day of your life,
old friend, how I would unwind it, paste
it together in a different collage,
back from the death car idling in the garage,
back up the stairs, your praying hands unlaced,
reassembling the bits of bread and tuna fish
into a ceremony of sandwich,
running the home movie backward to a space
we could be easy in, a kitchen place
with vodka and ice, our words like living meat.

Dear friend, you have excited crowds
with your example. They swell
like wine bags, straining at your seams.
I will be years gathering up our words,
fishing out letters, snapshots, stains,
leaning my ribs against this durable cloth
to put on the dumb blue blazer of your death.

STEPHAN DELBOS

Folding Her Corduroys

Tracing my thumb cuff upward on pinwales,
over the hole her bike's chain bit,
to thighs, like velvet, the ribs rubbed flat,

I think of an old stone staircase:
tarnished marble, blunted edges,
a furrow foot-worn in each step,

then lay the laundry, folded
in the darkness of a drawer.

We shape what we inhabit:
cloth, stone, the vessel of empty hands.

LYNNE SHAPIRO

Your Dead Mother

Dangles from the sky
Like a slim moon
Strung on a string
Silvery blue dress
Pleated like a curtain
Shimmers in your
Room at night
As cocktail gloves
And long fingers
Reach down to caress
Your sleepy head

MARIA TERRONE

Unmentionable

Buried
at the bottom of my lingerie drawer,
an antique, skin-toned wisp of silk
trimmed with lace and snapping shut
in complicated ways.

A frayed label says
Triangle Shirtwaist Company.

I cannot remember when or how
it came to be here.

I cannot see this confection without
seeing smoke, locked doors and fiery dives
through cruel, unmothering space.

Whose hands cut the silk,
sewed stitches so fine?
Did she hang by a thread for days
to die, or survive,
a wild-eyed girl-child?

This garment I will never wear
sears me, wails
from sachet-scented darkness.

MARGARET ATWOOD

White Cotton T-Shirt

White cotton T-shirt: an innocent garment then.
It made its way to us from the war, but we didn't know that.
For us it was the vestment of summer,
whiter than white, shining with whiteness
because it had been washed in blood, but we didn't know that,
and in the cropped sleeve, rolled up tightly
into a cuff, were tucked the cigarettes,
also white within their packet, also innocent,
as were white panties, white convertibles,
white-blond brush-cuts,
and the white, white teeth of the lilting smiles
of the young men.

Ignorance makes all things clean.
Our knowledge weighs us down.
We want it gone

so we can put on our white T-shirts
and drive once more through the early dawn
streets with the names we never could
pronounce, but it didn't matter,
over the broken glass and bricks, passing
the wary impoverished faces,
the grins filled with blackening teeth,
the starving dogs and stick children
and the slackened bundles of clothing
that once held men,
enjoying the rush of morning air
on our clean, tanned skins,
and the white, white flowers we hold out in our fists,
believing—still—that they are flowers of peace.

LESLEY WHEELER

Dressing Down, 1962

"Shalom," called the pink-shirted man in the Oceanic
Terminal of Heathrow, and I snapped,
"I do not want to talk to you." Manic

with fear, I extended one pointy-tipped shoe, tapped
the message home. My cases bulged with the wrong
clothes, every outfit trimmed with clipped

English, fit for the telephone jobs on Long
Island. Rwanda, Algeria, and me
declaring every kind of independence.

My skirt and I were green, not the pretty
pistachio that Jacqueline Kennedy wore,
but the color copper develops in the sea,

cold and unfortunate, the green of storms
that have never squalled before. My hat,
gloves, and I were pale, not plush like the warm

blonde women settling in their seats
and bubbling dipthongs to their husbands;
not even poignant, like the champagne satin

that Marilyn Monroe was buried in.
Just neutral, stale as a biscuit, off
as an old cup of milk. I was stubborn,

I would do what I said and leave
England. I would ride that El Al jet, mystery
novel in hand and never grieve.

Johnny Carson, the Jetsons, and me.
A new wardrobe in cartoon hues. Meanwhile,
my row-mate slipped off her court shoes, free

toes wiggling in hose. "We all went to Israel,
almost all of us on the flight, and are returning
to South Carolina," she explained in a drawl

that frightened me more than the turbofan
wailing beneath us. In her sundress, her stomach
looked soft. Ungirdled? Does everyone chat with a twang,

even the Jews? I do not want to talk,
but here I am, midair. "Coffee," I replied
to the hostess, slowly. I will never wear slacks,

but I can unfasten each word, open it wide.

KIM ADDONIZIO

"What Do Women Want?"

I want a red dress.
I want it flimsy and cheap,
I want it too tight, I want to wear it
until someone tears it off me.
I want it sleeveless and backless,
this dress, so no one has to guess
what's underneath. I want to walk down
the street past Thrifty's and the hardware store
with all those keys glittering in the window,
past Mr. and Mrs. Wong selling day-old
donuts in their café, past the Guerra brothers
slinging pigs from the truck and onto the dolly,
hoisting the slick snouts over their shoulders.
I want to walk like I'm the only
woman on earth and I can have my pick.
I want that red dress bad.
I want it to confirm
your worst fears about me,
to show you how little I care about you
or anything except what
I want. When I find it, I'll pull that garment
from its hanger like I'm choosing a body
to carry me into this world, through
the birth-cries and the love-cries too,
and I'll wear it like bones, like skin,
it'll be the goddamned
dress they bury me in.

Why I Cross-Dress

Because, for the moment, if I want, it will remind me I am not a man.
Because anatomy is not destiny.
A good woman is hard to find.
Because real men wear red plaid flannel shirts, not pastel silk blouses.
A silk gown smoothes my macho edges.
Because when I do, I will surprise my lover. She throws back her head, runs her fingers
      through her fine brown hair and sighs, "The colors don't match, and those
      five-inch stiletto heels are going to be hell on your ankles."
At Christmas I can deck the halls and don my gay apparel.
Because when I catwalk into a room, people smile and sip champagne, and when
      I stare into a mirror at the end of the hallway, I become pregnant with
      thought—I am not a woman, and when I exit the room, people put down
      their champagne glasses and murmur.
I really have nowhere to go. I cover my loneliness with a Merrywidow.
A bustier becomes my body armor; I cover my loneliness.
Still when I step out of the closet, for the moment, I become the other woman, and
      the only woman.   I'm not a man.   I'm not a woman.
So what if my car careened into a ditch? What would the emergency-room nurse say?
If she yanks the covers off, there I'll be in my chemise covering my father's
      shame.
At night I think about death, dying in my Maidenform bodysuit, found by
      the paramedics in the mid-afternoon, rigid as PVC, and slipped into a 100%
      silk body bag.

JAN BEATTY

When Foucault Entered the Body

My friend Aaron said he'd like to give Sean Penn
a tongue bath, & I guess that's clear enough,

but I want more. I want to wear men's shoes
because they're stylish, sturdy—& just because

I think Patricia Arquette's beautiful
doesn't mean I want to be her. Just give me a wife

beater & an AK-47 & I'll be Nic Cage
busting up Con-Air, fuckin A. You can call me

shallow, but in grad school the main theoryhead
called me late at night for advice about his boyfriend

& that's when Foucault entered the body—
give me a break with his "I'm not speaking" routine.

Nobody wants to inhabit his/her own body
all the time—Take my friend Aaron, for example.

When he's irritated, he says, "panties, panties, panties"
& that helps calm him down, & just because

my husband had to explain Popa Chubby, the blues singer,
to me—doesn't mean I'm naïve—just on vacation.

Why stay in the body & miss the ricochet back in,
the cool body return with its jolt of red sugar

& don't you just love the inside out of it?
The veins & pink slippery animal openings of it?

Panties, panties, panties.
When I dress in drag, honey, I'll be in a pink-flower-

prom-gown with a motherfuckin tiara—
because a sharkskin suit would be too much

like home.

Ziggurat Hat

The black and white stripes,
like taffeta steps, led
to a slanted black feather
plucked from a raven's wing.
The tip, stuck in the black
grosgrain band, was sharp
as a quill to write billets-doux;
the veil, little black glittery stars
caught in netting. Your eyes
were the color of Waterman's
blue ink. On windy days,
your lashes blackly coated
with cake mascara,
batted against the inblown veil.
In sunlight, dark stars were cast
on your rouged cheeks.
When you wore that hat,
men babbled as they spoke.
I, your daughter, holding
your gloved hand or the hem
of your three-quarter Persian
lamb coat, loved to look up at you
wearing that hat, or any other.

EILEEN MALONE

Eating Her Wedding Dress

Tossed over the vanity chair
delicious damp fingerprints
on my baby sister's white velvet gown
form small, new mushrooms

once again, I the old and unmarried
press my face to the wedding feast
eat pearls of pickled onions
raw oysters in tiny ivory shells

I release my tongue, lick salt
as spit squirts like estrogen
between emerging rat teeth
capable of grinding, chewing
this ceremony of thoughts
sliding all denial and neglect
like colorless afterbirth
down my slippery throat

I might seem old hag
devouring evidence
—what is left of the bride
what remains of my mind
—no matter, I no longer fear
I might be what I seem.

Selvage

On a clumsy native loom
She wove a clever fabric, working words
In red on a white ground to tell the tale

—Ovid, *Metamorphoses*, Tale of Philomela
translated by A. D. Melville.

CAROL GUESS

Hem

Hems caress fishnets, thighs scissoring asphalt for a breakout run. Hems come undone. Tug on a hem and the whole dress unravels. Hem a burnt sleeve and the house catches fire. *The house is on fire! Put it out with a hem!* Fabric no one has the guts to name. Untamed chafing. What rises first. Every weak sister knows that taffeta itches. Hem a sentence as a seamstress edits.

My Grandmother's Suit

My grandmother wears
a blue wool suit she'd sewn
but not quite finished.
Raw selvages visible,
silk lining dangling
from the tailored jacket,
collar still in her workbox.
It was cut precisely
to a difficult pattern.
She'd always been proud
of her craft, but now she's
letting us see how much
had gone into it,
the inglorious underside.
She says she'd run out of time,
she'd rather be unfinished
than ready-made.

ANN WALTERS

Zen and the Art of Knitting Socks

Form the gusset into shape with a nip here, a tuck there;
an origamic folding over of the universe
until the stars can touch their toes.

Heels are a mystery unsolvable, like the rhythmic
fellowship of needles and yarn,
like knowing strangers in a shop full of wool.

Accept that you must turn when you are told,
must pick up and hold the hidden joints
that bend your will to a higher purpose.

Leave the toe seam till last because it feels so good
to pleasure your fingers back and forth
across that swollen line.

Let the pattern of ribbing indented into your pale ankle
speak for itself after the sock has been peeled away.
Wear your stripes with pride.

VALERIE LAWSON

Warm, At Last

I made my song a coat
                    —W. B. Yeats

I sat by myself at the start of the reading, draped my coat across
the empty seat next to me and buried my nose in a book.
My mind played musical chairs, moved people around
as if playing one of those hand-held games, the one with
the tiles and one blank space. There is always one blank space.

The seat beside me stayed empty. I pretended the seat
belonged to the woman two seats over. Thinking
this made it so.

There was a beautiful woman looking for a place to sit,
prowling tiger-bright in the aisles. I was sure I had stolen
her seat, frightened away the dragon due to fall from the sky.

The reading began.

The sighs and wordless understandings that could have been
shared gathered up the coat from the empty chair, fleshed it out,
poked arms through the sleeves, legs from the bottom,
sidled its way into the aisle and disappeared.

When the reading was over, the crowd shuffled in line,
open books waiting to be signed. The poet spelled my name
correctly, without prompting, a perfect stranger.

On the train ride home, I squeezed between two filled seats,
pretended the passengers knew each other, elbows and thighs
touching. Warm at last, I pulled a book from my pocket,
opened it to a blank page and wrote this poem.

BILLY COLLINS

Taking Off Emily Dickinson's Clothes

First, her tippet made of tulle,
easily lifted off her shoulders and laid
on the back of a wooden chair.

And her bonnet,
the bow undone with a light forward pull.

Then the long white dress, a more
complicated matter with mother-of-pearl
buttons down the back,
so tiny and numerous that it takes forever
before my hands can part the fabric,
like a swimmer's dividing water,
and slip inside.

You will want to know
that she was standing
by an open window in an upstairs bedroom,
motionless, a little wide-eyed,
looking out at the orchard below,
the white dress puddled at her feet
on the wide-board, hardwood floor.

The complexity of women's undergarments
in nineteenth century America
is not to be waved off,
and I proceeded like a polar explorer
through clips, clasps, and moorings,
catches, straps, and whalebone stays,
sailing toward the iceberg of her nakedness.

Later, I wrote in a notebook
it was like riding a swan into the night,
but, of course, I cannot tell you everything—

the way she closed her eyes to the orchard,
how her hair tumbled free of its pins,
how there were sudden dashes
whenever we spoke.

What I can tell you is
it was terribly quiet in Amherst
that Sabbath afternoon,
nothing but a carriage passing the house,
a fly buzzing in a windowpane.

So I could plainly hear her inhale
when I undid the very top
hook-and-eye fastener of her corset

and I could hear her sigh when finally it was unloosed,
the way some readers sigh when they realize
that Hope has feathers,
that reason is a plank,
that life is a loaded gun
that looks right at you with a yellow eye.

JOHN ESTES

A few chemicals mixed together and flesh and blood and bone just fade away!

I, too, am an invisible man.
But what amazes Claude Rains
ho-hums an age of evaporation.
The wonder is that, unlike me—
so embarrassed by particularity—
he persists as a man of action.
He's a dashing and brilliant killer.
Limpid as a windexed window
his footsteps slurp, his rocking chair
creaks while a lit cigarette
dances in midair. He evades the rap
of most vapors; I am a thought
trapped thinking. If there's a virtue
to diaphany, in the practice of
wrapping my head over and over again
until I get the eyeholes right
so my friends can see me,
it's the dispersal of racial shame
over my body's inmost secret
workings: how I now revel in japery,
like entering a room, my robes
discarded, with a stomach
full of chewed food. Li-Young Lee
cautioned me to restrain
this impulse toward the clever.
He told me a poem is like a bowl
of pudding: you have to stir and stir
and stir, whip it until it's smooth.
He says this making wide swirling
counter-clockwise motions

in a big, imaginary bowl of pudding.
A gaping hole in the elbow
of his cable-knit baggy sweater
sways over this concoction;
it's this memory's essential detail.

M. J. IUPPA

Bleach

A speck. No bigger
than the head of a pin.

                Bright.
I can see through it,
like a knot-hole.

Like a beacon, it shines
                a distance
on this shirt.

Bleach, you say, touching
                the spot
                just above
                my heart.

SUSAN MEYERS

footnotes, an annotation

[1] *Goody two-shoes,* overly cheerful
    person who started out
        with one shoe but now has two.
    And they match, goody, goody.

[2] *Pigeon-toed,* first used in 1801.
    Scandalous,
        those red sandals
    (T-strapped and buckled) pinching
    the tender grass
          barely.

[3] The foot has 26 bones, one fewer than the hand.
    So what, if sneakers
        kick their way down the trail,
    tatting up   old leaves?

[4] Achilles, unpopular name for a dog.
    From hearth to snow (see also *ice*)
    fur-lined clogs   click
    their soles, toggle on
            and off.

[5] *Toehold,* a wrestling move.
    Hip boots, tough enough to battle
    surprise—
        say, a wakening
    of snakes.

CHRISTINA LOVIN

Girl in a Red Hat

She wore red shoes, the girl in a red hat, and nothing else.
I found her beautiful, released her from the thick sheaf
of artfully nude photographs in rather prim poses—
my father's samples for calendars he sold to be pinned
to the walls of men's clubs, auto shops, and back rooms
of bars. I nailed her to the wall of the chicken shed, admired
her creamy flesh, the color of a Rhode Island Red egg.
She dimpled at her hips and cheeks and knees, blushed
where rosy nipples bloomed from behind the proper slope
of those precise globes of her breasts. She was flawless but
for the harsh creases that ran the width and length of the print
where it had been folded to make her fit with her sisters
inside the sample case, her perfection spoiled with crackling ink,
crow's feet of the slick white paper beneath revealed.
Over and over I ran my palm across the paper, the wallboards
of the henhouse rough beneath my hand, futilely trying
to smooth her wrinkled skin, that crazing paper smile.

Shimmer and Shield

Droll shade and lace protection. Veil that keeps
my gaze in place. Frippery cloche—*peau de soie*—

a single leaf; some buckram and net transforming
the view—the almond of the eye (no, rounder),

its black mascara'd hedging edge. Let's pretend
that time is dead. The world shifts in the white

flirtatious chinks. Wrestle the tiny, toothed
combs grown deep in the skull.

DANIEL W.K.LEE

Ties

I am looking for irony among
these lengths of silk
stitched with Italian surnames,
trademarks of English refinement,
and sentimentalities ready to be loosened
like the half-Windsor knots
I'd abandon for one last turn
at hanging about your neck.

—*to C. L.*

ISHMAEL VON HEIDRICK-BARNES

Florence

i left my suitcase
in Florence
because it was large
and i did not know how to travel

i like to think
an Italian boy
is wearing the button-down shirt
left inside the luggage

i close my eyes
and he's pulling a pack of cigarettes
from the front pocket,
sleeves slapping wind wordless

The Palazzo Vecchio
stamping its imprimatur
on the color
of cloth

It is possible
in this inferno of city
to live
two separate lives

ANDY WASS

The Fitting

Look into number 6. That blown scarf is bird-flocks
that weave through the wind and split the seams of light.
Tatted blue jay swatches fly with parrot greens
and dartings of yellow finch.
   —Rod Jellema

Designers are the perverts, or
else they just don't know:
slices, panes,
organs of clothing—
they are our best secrets:
         not a leg, but its cover;
         not a hip, but its shaping;
         not a part, but its mooring.

Pretty swarmings
in baskets, in drawers,
on nakeds—skinned—are sketches:
the way to recover
         reshape
      to wing;
      to moor
a kiss: a loosed-lace shoe.

CLAIRE ZOGHB

Living in Bodies

After a week of hospital visits—
a loved one's cracked hip,
an accidental glimpse of another's
colostomy bag, wasted legs
and bedsores, and an old friend's
trinity of fractured ribs—

I'm thinking of our own brittle heart-cages
and mourn the cruel loss of what
we believe is *independence:*

how we drape the flimsy
hospital gown of denial around
our fragile bodies—

believe a single knot
at the nape is enough
to hold, to prevent
a flapping open behind
our borrowed backs—

never realizing it was sewn
to survive only so many
washings, so much bleach.

Inheritance

I
am the
woman they give
dead women's
clothes to
I live easily   grass-green
in them, my   zebras loosed
friend's mother's   in ivory
print dress with   space
or
my own
mother's
bracelet:
her opalescent
hearts clasp
my wrist   the continuing
comfort-   significance of
ably I   dead women's
can never   shoes even
outwalk   the cold
I
wrap out
with the autumn
orange wool
of an
inherit-
ed
coat   wardrobe
mine   of chance
is the   of well-
worn
inevitability
none other
suits

In the locker room

I surprise the women
dressed in their bodies: in breasts,
knees, eyebrows, pubic
hair. Excitable children appear
to accept them. Pitted and fat, dazzling
and golden, the women
drowse under the shower, a preview of
bodies the children try on
with their eyes.

At sixty-five, I am less than
a child, whose mother walked
fearfully clothed, afraid of the water.
My grip on the towel gives me away. I move
into the pool suitably over my head
past my mother's responsible
daughter. Later, wild to learn, I practice
standing alone—only my underpants on—
under the gun
of the hair dryer.

A queen-size woman
sweetly accosts me, recommends
more clothes. Someone has pointed out
a peek-a-boo crack in the men's
locker room. "What a shame," she intones,
"such a nice clean
club." I loiter in my underwear
worn out with surveillance.
What we don't know
won't hurt us.

Oh, but it does deprive us!
These ravenous mermaids,
stripped to their scales, swim from
the framed reproductions, pale and diaphanous
planes engineered for unmistakable
languor. Something has changed
in the changing room where we step out of
lingerie meant for the fainting couch
and bring on the body in person.

JEAN HOLLANDER

To Clotho, in care of Sears

Sears has a money-back guarantee
for any merchandise, you don't even
have to speak, just shove the stuff
across the counter and the cash
register returns whatever it cost
plus tax.
                    Dear Clotho, long ago I got
a faulty pattern and bad goods.
I tried to knit myself a fitting garment but
it's tight in the left armpit, slack
on top, clings to the butt and wrinkles
at the crotch.
                    I want my life back,
full refund or a credit slip
to crawl back out of it and sew
a new elastic skintight cycling stretch outfit
in purple/red/plum orange/green hallucinogenic synthesis
but I suspect not even Sears takes back
that unskeined stretch of stubborn wool
I knotted, knit.

Dreamboat

(Thinking of Marilyn Monroe
after viewing Magritte's white dress
in *Philosophy in the Boudoir*)

So here she comes again,
that big blonde dreamboat
sailing onto the scene,
polished to a sheen,
heady and haloed by seabirds,
sails at her mast billowing
like a finger crooked
and calling you to her.

And you move toward her,
just on the chance
she may ask you to enter
some cabin holding
a geography of mounds
in breasts and buttocks,
and where in the closet hangs
a perfect white dress,

dreaming her body
breathing inside it.

LAURA MADELINE WISEMAN

My Imaginary Cock Dresses for Halloween

Holy the cocks of the grandfathers of Kansas!
—Allen Ginsberg

My imaginary cock mans the bedroom's closet.
My cock pitches costumes: a Renaissance frock,
a wand capped with a star, a fairy princess skirt,
a witch's conical hat and bodice laced in webs.
I'll find the perfect thing for us, my cock says.

I sit criss-cross on the feather mattress and toy
with a satin garter and thigh-high seamed tights.
I catch a ruby slipper lobbed from the hope chest.
I could be Dorothy, I say and tug from the pile
a blue jumper with a blouse snug at the neck.

My imaginary cock says, *No, you can't be her.*
We've got to match and I'm going as a weapon.
From a crate I yank out a coiffed auburn do.
Please, I beg. I scamper to the make-up trove
and return with a fire-engine red lipstick.

My cock says, *Absolutely not. I can't be*
a bayonet in the Emerald City. Nor can I be
a cannon on the yellow brick road. How can I be
a handgun in Oz? My cock emerges girdled
in crinoline, cowboy boots, and a mustache.

I open the armoire for a pair of bobby socks.
Listen, I say, *It will be fun.* I assemble
my Halloween garb on our comforter.
I hum the 1939 film's classic theme song.
I'll be that Kansas gal and you can be her Toto.

Washing Moon

Under her serge dress, those are her briny ankles

Every full moon she washes her knives in the sea
to keep them sharp

She hones each blade on the sandy sole of her foot

With a hot mouthful of straight-pins,
she is pinning a lace collar of tatting and openwork

to the full slope of her bodice
It swells and falls like foam on water

Before her, sea wrack and one lost fork
whoosh and retreat with the casual pebbles

                  Tonight in a blue town
she will dine with that fork,

its barnacles and tines salty as blood,
and beside her, at table,

in the place of a husband, these long-handled knives

SUSAN YOUNT

Socks of Fire

Never mind that the manager instructed you to wear solid black or navy
socks. *Hey little pistol.* You'll even forget the four fat fucks at table five.
Want to make some extra cash? You got the round table tonight and in
these smokin' socks you'll serve chicken-fried-steak, mashed potatoes
and sawmill gravy scintillatingly. *Let me be your pepper you salty
centerfold.* You. The star of the Cracker Barrel Ballet and Roadside
Freak Show. Your Glowing-Charcoal Argyle Socks (No. 555), dyed in
China, will stay mid-calf as you dance to the tune of cranky, deep-fried
okra. *What time you get off work? I'm staying at the hotel next door.*
Even that 50-cent tip left by the two old crones is no match for these
swanky Uzbekistan-combustible-cotton, hand-quilted socks. *Another cup
of coffee hon.* Your patrons will be amazed as you blaze through kitchen
grease seizing oversized portions of mac and cheese for their delight.
More biscuits. More cornbread. Then, sparks flickering from your
ankles—the manager notices. You are fired. You're secretly thrilled. He
calls you into his office. You take a seat. Kick off your shoes. Light a
cigarette from your hand-linked heel.

Ribbed, stay-up tops. Made by India's leading hosiery-maker to the
upper caste. $32. Glowing-Charcoal Argyle Socks (No. 555), as
described, combustible-cotton, originally found in hell.

MARY LANGER THOMPSON

My First Pink Slip

Not a lacy half or whole
silk of lingerie, but
a sheer missive
delivered today, needing
my unfashionable signature
saying I received it, not
that I agree not to cling
to a position gone.

The smooth Board decided
in private session,
secret even to Victoria,
taking action pursuant
to code section 44951
to unclasp me.

Four a.m. I awake
under a rusty moon
in a cold-hot sweat,
neglected in my negligee
drenched in worry.
I've finally been noticed.

Sheer

The soul was not cured,
it was as full as a clothes closet
of dresses that did not fit.

—Anne Sexton, "The God—onger"

AMY MacLENNAN

Lures

It happened three times,
my dangle earring hooked
to your beard, a clean
catch.
     I've changed
to hoops now,
we come away
without a snag.
     And still
I feel the pull: my face
tugged back to yours,
a line between us
tight.

CHARLOTTE NEKOLA

Trapeze Song

Roscoe, Roscoe, I say, catch me,
but you say fly with your eyes closed,
and all the dogs in their Queen Elizabeth collars
will sit up and wave.
Suddenly, the bareback riders stop quarreling.
The citizens of Toledo gasp at once,
hold their hats and hems,
and see themselves in plumes
as they wheel their bodies again
and again across empty space and hope
that someone will catch their wrists.
Below, the beds of sawdust shift.
Roscoe, you caught me, I say afterward,
but you say no, you caught me,
and we toast each other with schnapps and pork chops,
still wrapped in our robes, shining like trouts,
as another solid town and city hall
wash past our window. Our breathing behind us,
our sleeves lift.

Absorbed

While her breathing
head and hair welled
on my side of the pillow,
my pants swelled on the table.

While her mossy gown
shook over and down to soak up
the glossy half of both of us
in fire thickly attended, my pants

put this all in perspective, half
dripping from the table, extended
when sudden light and wind prodded
movement with her breathing,

upended till my head and hair
and the light and the wind were
seething from the fire flicking
both of us into flames that subsided only

when my longstanding obligation
to my pants was faithfully fulfilled. And
the light and the wind divided.
And I never saw that table again.

ERIC HOWARD

To Sacks, a Costumer

The dead tell the living
play your part well, for the fashion

of your world is passing.
To be remembered,

remember you have no choice
when she puts the spool

of your life on her spindle
and its thread through her machine.

You want the story to start there
but it's not even the story,

which starts in the rain with a woman
walking down a street in a 40s

raincoat with hidden buttons,
in tears because she's lost

and soaked from scarf to pumps,
who steps in an icy puddle

in front of a good looking guy,
size 40 trench coat, and the fedora

without the bullet hole.
That's where the story starts,

with the studio rain that's from
a river that rose from steam

over seas through goats
and presidents and the dead,

that's immortal like one
who listens to a song

in her head as she keeps
her eye on the blurry needle

and the scene where two fools meet
plays like a movie in her mind.

She knows her silk confections
will be ruined by the water

in all the mortal fluids
that are knotted to each other, even as

her hands flow, sewing a seam.
She isn't distant or cold. She's just behind the scenes.

ALDA MERINI

The Apron

My mother, though, had an old apron
for holidays and work,
and she consoled herself with it by living.
We found solace in that apron
that was given away to the ragmen
after her death, but a tramp,
recognizing its maternity,
made a soggy pillow from it
for his living funeral rites.

—*translated by Susan Stewart*

Diapers for My Father

Pads or pull-ons—that
is the question. Whether to buy
pads dangled from straps
fastened with buttons or Velcro—
pads rising like a bully's cup
stiff as pommel with stickum backs
to stick in briefs. Or, dear God,
the whole thing rubberized,
size 38 in apple green, with
or without elastic leg. Or the kind,
I swear, with an inside pocket
to tuck a penis in—little resume
in a folder. Old mole, weeping
his one eye out at the tunnel's end.

The clerk is nothing but patience
practiced with sympathy.
Her eyes soak up everything.
In ten minutes she's my cotton batting,
my triple panel, triple shield—my Depends
against the hour of the mop: skeleton
with a sponge mouth dry as a grinning brick
waiting in the closet.

She carries my choices to the register,
sighing the floor with each step.
I follow, absorbed away to nothing.

How could Hamlet know what flesh is heir to?
Ask Claudius, panicky in his theft,
hiding in the garden where it all began
or behind the arras, stuffing furbelows

from Gertrude's old court dress into his codpiece.
Or better, ask Ophelia, daughter too
of a foolish, mean-mouthed father,
who launched herself like a boat of blotters
only to be pulled babbling under the runaway stream.

ELIZABETH DANSON

Protective Clothing Required

Time's apron shrugs off the dirty work;
its pockets are roomy, set in ordered rows.
The lower ones are huge, their labels rubbed
and handled, mostly blurred and gone. Even Time
has forgotten their contents. The fabric holds up
though, under amazing pressure; it's a miracle
how it throws off stains, even blood eventually.
And Time stays pristine, each new moment
stainless, undisturbed.
The apron's for what happens next.

ANNE HARDING WOODWORTH

Undershirt

Ribbed white cotton
it had a deep round neck
and a place for arms
to emerge long,
the left one tanned
from hanging out the car window,
and a stretchable place
where his heart thumped
up to the moment it couldn't any more,
just after he'd said the air
was heavy that morning
and rain would ease
the difficult weight
and bring a fresh scent
through its transparency.
Cellophane wrapped
the last one in his drawer,
new, with the price
sticking to a corner.

VASILIKI KATSAROU

Portmanteau

Something green
the length of my body
has dropped off my body

Arms without
arms

Seams
torn

My overcoat
lies
upon your vacant gray

Eyes like loose buttons

CARLOS HERNÁNDEZ PEÑA

Cold Mud Question

A wild winter
sculpts
an open coffin
at an airport—
a warning
wrapped up
in cellophane—
an orphan
in a waiting room,
a promise
filled with dread.

Snow will call
tomorrow
for high
black leather
boots.

Today, how could I bury
this frozen mud view,
and not think
         about winter
again   ever?

SHELLEY SPENCE KIERNAN

A Dead Woman's Dress

Something proffered, held out
like the star moss of grief or history
an old skin

I ask if it will fit
with a tribesman's mistrust
of the worn

This woman's death
is a gray dress
passed hand to hand

ROBERTA P. FEINS

Un-costumed Love

After a long day together,
you smell like me: smoke,
traffic, lavender we brushed
in the park. In our bedroom,

I empty your pockets of tissues,
parking tickets, love letters,
lift the tiny vestigial wings
of your collar, fondle

pearl buttons like pesky pennies.
First, the top neck-squeezer,
drill sergeant, then the shyer
lower ones delicately,

one-by-one undone.
Finally your malleable torso
loosens, releases my head,
hands, hips. My finger

through the reinforced loop
at your neck, I swing
your angelic flutter through the air
then turn aside, leave you

limp and gasping on the floor.

Freed Up

He said I had nice ones, even though I'd always thought they were so little, but why did I bind them up? One day I left my bra in the drawer. All day could feel the feel of them. Couldn't forget they were there. Felt good just leaning down to throw a wad of paper in the trash. And standing up, nipples like third and fourth eyes, looking straight out at whoever was coming toward me in the long hall. Looking clear inside. Into secrets, hiding places. Until they were out for good, out of the muffled fiber-filled shells, elastic tightenings, hard-wire frames. Like bare green leaves unfolding in April, swelling as they opened. Leisurely, soft, brushing into a hand.

NADINE D. BOULWARE

Steppin

I am laced up,
   tied, snapped, zipped.
Sometimes I step in gum
   mud, spit, crap, water.
I am shined, polished and dyed.

There are times when your feet stink,
   your socks rub me the wrong way
   and pets chew on me.

After all of that, you are
   my only way out of the house.

RACHIM BASKIN

Forsythia, you floozy!
Prising focus from your older sisters—
Snowdrop White and
Purple Crocus.

Buxom bloom!
First to flaunt a summer dress
(a fuck-me yellow one no less)
fully knowing the effect on us.

Yes, lily has a beauty more mature;
rose, aromatic allure;
and lilac, *l'haute couture*

but only you are pinned up in

the greenhouse of desire.

MEGAN BUCHANAN CHERRY

Spring in the First Floor Women's Bathroom at Northern Arizona University

What a shame to zip
French cherry-blossomed panties
back into work pants.

Wish I could cartwheel,
just cotton hiphuggers, boots,
white linoleum.

DEIRDRE BRENNAN

The Blue Dress

(Henri Matisse)

He had to hate her to paint her
out of existence,
to cancel her out, imprison her
within great folds of cloth

voluminous sleeves
and rhapsody of frills
flouncing at the neck
elating the bodice
cascading in arabesques to hem.

Did he love her once
then froze her in this room
at some unclean time
lest at her touch
his world might fall to pieces?

And now he is master,
her nothingness complete.
The dress bubbles and flows
from compliant shoulders,
her hand a starfish in its depths.

JOHN L. FALK

Clothes and Power

To shed clothing for a woman
Is to don dominion,
Every garment fabricated
To hint of its heavenly absence.
Hesitant perhaps,
Or luxuriant with limbs
Tracked alike by greybeard
And schoolboy: it makes no difference.
This is the only power
Expending will increase.

Strip insignia from a man,
His indexed place, affiliation,
And he shivers foolish,
Though it be the tropics.
Without team-lettered cap, equally
Declarative shirt, he is faceless
As a brutish rock, an oiled pebble
Shifted by every beachfront tide.
Imagine a bare-assed army,
Each man ordering arms stark naked:
You couldn't fight for laughing.

A naked woman with a pen knife
Could rip the day or night sky
Open with a shrug, or the slightest
Flexing of her wrist.
A shoulder movement, praise be,
Insinuates ensuing avalanche.
We cannot even discuss
Her hands reaching up
To gather in her hair.

The Little Black Dress

1. Shopping

The woman steps back, cocks her head and inspects
the three-way mirror: two of them draped
on her body and clothes flung everywhere.

And those other women whisper back to her
what to want and which to choose—*the little
black dress, little black dress, little black
dress* tells her what to do:

> *Slip into it*
> *Press little flat breasts*
> *into the padded black bustier*
> *Zip up the long black back zipper*
> *Show off your shoulders   Become*
> *your better self   five pounds thinner*
> *an inch more*

which is what she wants, so why not
buy into the feeling: readymade and womanly just now.

2. Night Out

The little black dress goes to cocktail parties—
orders something with milk in it, *like maybe
a White Russian.* The little black dress titters
and flirts:

> *Really?*
> *Oh how interesting!*
> *You're so very clever.*

Men desire the little black dress, want to
eye what's underneath. Their martinis
with triple olives hafted on tiny swords hover
in small swells. Anyman takes her home,
drives her there in his red sports car.
The little black dress cracks open
like a velvet clamshell. The two of them blur,
kissing themselves into extinction.

3. Morning, Woman Alone

The dress lies
sunken in the corner
like a naughty child
nevertheless still croons
her siren song:

> *I will surround you*
> *in sweetness and surety,*
> *whatever is wanted*
> *I will be. I'll make you*
> *soft and sultry.*
> *I am the best excuse.*

Naked, the woman pours herself a scotch,
slips into a terry robe, *dis-* no
*un*believes everything
the man with olives has said.

The blackness is gone now, her mind
clear, the voices quiet. The woman
is beautiful, brimming with intent.

Closet Space

I haven't decided what to wear,
my closet seeming plagiarized
from some other life—the lime halter
dress I doffed in New Orleans, the burnt
orange tube top with Zodiac brooch,
ruffled zebra print, white linen
pinked in the wash. I barely know myself
through these—what floors they'd slept on,
while I thrashed in some bed,
or who may have brushed against them
once in a supermarket, buying quince
and white wine. My boyfriend tugs
at the sleeve of his shirt, cuffing
the ends to the elbow. He is wearing
the same blue shirt he was when I met him.
I almost tell him this. But then what pasts
do we have really?

LINDA ANNAS FERGUSON

Sundown

I have decided.
I will leave barefoot,
not even a suitcase,
shoes under your table.

We sit straight, poised,
our shadows stretch stiff
across the floor.
I drink a last cup of light

and remember how we
watched the coming night,
forced the days to come and go.

But now, when the dark
presses flat against our window,
we lie naked on the bed,

our clothes in the closet,
bodiless.

Taking Back the Bra Drawer

I started by giving away, slowly, the left side—
first the top of the dresser, where there was
always a pile of his clothes—workman's pants,
long-sleeved tie-dyes. There is still a handcrafted belt,
heavy with an eagle buckle. Then I tucked
his laundry—clean—into the bra drawer.
Donated the impulse buys to the Salvation Army
to make room for his khaki cargo shorts,
grey thermal bottoms. The solid heaviness
of a man crowded out the florals and polka dots.
His scent—patchouli and work—is worn into
the flannel bedding I bought to keep us through winter.
A hockey puck of mint snuff rests on the carpet
next to the bed. He is everywhere—his
tape measurer keeps the kitchen counter from
escaping. And yet—after a normal argument—
when I suggested he stay at his place tonight—
and he decided to stay there for all nights—
I want him here to the degree
of absenting myself. I will be any woman—
one who hasn't slept with other women, or
who hasn't been married before—one who will
sew by hand until she is needle-pricked dry.
I don't want him to be another man—
another box of leftover belongings in a closet
waiting to be picked up,
another man whose name I use to describe
a period in my life,
another man whose jewelry rests in a hidden
drawer, worn only as an accessory to
regret. Another man whose children
will not giggle when I balloon sky-blue
cotton sheets against the ceiling.

Jane Deals with Infidelity

—For J. M.

She cuts his ties in half,
hangs them over chairs, towel rods,
the doorknobs he cocked silently
while she lay watching in the dark
wide awake.

She cuts them to a raw, sharp edge,
they fall from her fists
like tongues, smooth as silk
though she knows they are not.
Like whispers they are beautiful

and false. In each design she finds
a hidden pattern: a checked past
delicately woven that shimmered undetected
for years. A flaw that ran the full length
of him. And so she cuts them up

mid-phrase, drapes them from the couch,
kitchen drawers, windowsills that trap
the evening breeze. At times she sees
them move, hears them mouth the same
cool lies:

imperfections, they claim, *are not flaws;*
they add to the beauty of the fabric,
and mixture of texture
is desired. Durability,
they swear, *is not affected.*

The Hofburg Imperial Palace, Vienna

It took days for Empress Elisabeth's
tresses to dry, the guide tells us
describing her portrait.

I see her exercise room
and riding attire. She was a fanatic
about staying slim.

The Empress was fifty-two
when her son died—making us
some kind of sisters. She became

especially restless, traveling constantly.

I study the photo of her dress
worn to Geneva—the nipped-in waist
a man's hands could cage,

the tear where the assassin's knife went in.

ELIZABETH H. BARBATO

Stiletto Blue

after Mark Tansey's The Key

Is the brightest star in his oily mouth.
Look at her shake, tap, wiggle, spur on
his hand, clutch keys, the slick lock.

Turning in skilled mirrors, foxed old
as the Medici, she steams open envelopes,
x-rays white dresses in newsprint falsettos.

Whoever paid for her this time
probably should have asked for a receipt.
She demands a Borgia ring, thin crinoline,

and shocks both Eros and Thanatos
with behavior at their banquet.
While falling through an escalator,

her heels link and catch:
dangling, she negotiates.
Crossing bridges, she's a spider blade,

balancing in the sound of a negligee.
Whether or not he has the key, she'll get in.
Listen: it's Ms. Crooked, *chaussure a cric.*

DIANE LOCKWARD

Eve's Red Dress

I hang
deep in her closet,
red
as any apple she's ever bitten.

She wants to slip
into me. Her mother's voice says, *No.*
Red is not your color, not good
with your hair, your face, your eyes.
Her mother would dress her in blue,
but she's been blue so long. I shimmer
and sparkle, the perfect size
and luscious.

She reaches for me,
imagines how I would slide onto her
like skin. She knows she would be
sensational in me. She longs for my satin,
my deep neckline, my thin straps, rope of black
pearls around her neck.

She wants
to go dancing in me—tango, bossa nova,
merengue—my skirt fanning out like brushfire,
her mother's words smouldering in ashes, wants
to burst like a fireball onto the floor, spinning
and whirling, my skirt singing, *Touch me and burn.*

JANE KNECHTEL

Cardinal

Late summer.
I come upon a red bra
dangling out the upstairs
window of a house like
a revolutionary flag.
It's unexpected—
like midlife.
Cheeky as a tattoo;
an exotic bird
fluttering in the
evening light.
I drive on.

All winter
in the gray rain
that red bra—
stubborn,
hungry,
pecking.

J. D. SMITH

Sweater

This wool is the closest I can come
to the distant fold's
fellow-feeling, winter warmth.

But I may yet know
a claw's election,
the raw entry of teeth.

Everywhere, wolves must be fed.

LYNN EMANUEL

The White Dress

What does it feel like to be this shroud
on a hanger, this storm cloud hanging
in the closet? We itch to feel it, it itches
to be felt, it feels like an itch—

encrusted with beading, it's an eczema
of sequins, rough, gullied, riven,
puckered with stitchery, a frosted window
against which we long to put our tongues,

a vase for holding the long-stemmed
bouquet of a woman's body.
Or it's armor and it fits like a glove.
The buttons run like rivets down the front.

When we're in it we're machinery,
a cutter nosing the ocean of a town.
Right now it's lonely locked up
in the closet; while we're busy

fussing at our vanity, it hangs there
in the drooping waterfall of itself,
a road with no one on it, bathed
in moonlight, rehearsing its lines.

ACKNOWLEDGMENTS

The editors wish to thank the generous poets and publishers who granted permission to use the poems, and to our patient families for allowing us the time to devote to this project. Special thanks to Jean Foos, Shelley Kiernan, Tony Lutkus, Dirk Rowntree, and Arlene Weiner for their help and advice.

Grateful acknowledgment is made to the publications from which some of the poems were chosen. Unless specifically noted otherwise, copyright of the poems is held by the individual poets.

Kim Addonizio: "'What Do Women Want?'" from *Tell Me* by Kim Addonizio, © 2000 by Kim Addonizio. Reprinted with permission of BOA Editions Ltd.

Sherrill Alesiak: "Hanging Clothes" was originally published on line at www.2River.org. Then it appeared in print in *the 2River View*, Fall 2006.

Margaret Atwood: "White Cotton T-Shirt" from *The Door: Poems by Margaret Atwood.* © 2007 by O.W. Toad Ltd. Reprinted by permission of Houghton Mifflin Harcourt Publishing Company. All rights reserved.

Wendy Barker: "Freed Up" from *New York Quarterly.* Also forthcoming in *Nothing Between Us*: *The Berkeley Years* (Del Sol Press, 2009).

Jan Beatty: "When Foucault Entered the Body" from *Red Sugar* by Jan Beatty. © 2008 by Jan Beatty. Reprinted by permission of the University of Pittsburgh Press.

Deirdre Brennan: "The Blue Dress" from *Beneath Castles of White Sail* (Divas Series, Arlen House, Galway, 2003).

Billy Collins: "Taking Off Emily Dickinson's Clothes" from *Picnic, Lightning* by Billy Collins, © 1998 by Billy Collins. Reprinted by permission of the University of Pittsburgh Press.

Carolyn A. Dahl: "Cutting Cloth for Rag Rugs" was previously published in the 2008 *Women Artists Datebook* (Syracuse Cultural Workers Press, Syracuse, NY).

Diane Elayne Dees: "The New Recruits" was originally published in *Umbrella* (Winter 2006).

Madeline DeFrees: "In the locker room" from *Possible Sibyls* by Madeline DeFrees (Lynx House Press, 1991). By permission of Eastern Washington University Press and the author.
Lynn Emanuel: "The White Dress" from *Then, Suddenly—* by Lynn Emanuel, © 1999 by Lyn Emanuel. Reprinted by permission of the University of Pittsburgh Press.

Elaine Equi: "Armani Weather" from *Ripple Effect: New and Selected Poems* by Elaine Equi, © 1998 by Elaine Equi. Reprinted with permission of Coffee House Press.

John L. Falk: "Clothes and Power" from *Snow and Other Guises* (Guernica, 2000). © 2000 by John L. Falk and Guernica Editions Inc.

Linda Annas Ferguson: "Sundown" from *Last Chance to Be Lost* (Kentucky Writers Coalition, 2003).

Alice Friman: "Diapers for My Father" from *The Ohio Review*, *57*, republished in *The Ohio Review Thirtieth Anniversary: New & Selected*, in 2000.

Christine Gelineau: "Inheritance" first appeared in *The Beloit Poetry Journal*, *43* (Spring 1993).

Wally Glickman: "Makinglove" from *Some Rhymes for the Times* by Wally Glickman (waglick press, 2001). © 2001 by Wally Glickman.

Jorie Graham: "San Sepolcro" from *Erosion* by Jorie Graham (Princeton University Press, 1983). © 1983 by Princeton University Press.

Daniel A. Harris: "Attire" from a longer version in *Loose Parlance* by Daniel A. Harris, © 2008 Daniel A. Harris. By permission of Ragged Sky Press.

Ishmael von Heidrick-Barnes: "Florence" was previously published in *The Poetry Conspiracy* (April 2001).

Jean Hollander: "To Clotho, In Care of Sears" from *Organs and Blood* by Jean Hollander. © 2008 David Robert Books, Cincinnati, Ohio.

Janis Butler Holm: "If Paris Hilton Wrote Poetry" originally appeared in *Maisonneuve*, *10* (August/September 2004).

M. J. Iuppa: "Bleach" first appeared in *Buckle &*, and later in *Night Traveler* (Foothills Publishing, 2003).

Vasiliki Katsarou: "Portmanteau" originally appeared in *wicked alice* (Summer 2007).

James Keane: "Absorbed" from *The Real Eight View*, *11* (e-zine, November 4, 2006).

Jane Knechtel: "Cardinal" from *Tar Wolf Review*, *3* (Winter/Spring 2005).

Maxine Kumin: "How It Is" from *Selected Poems 1960–1990* by Maxine Kumin, © 1978 by Maxine Kumin. Used by permission of W.W. Norton & Company, Inc.

Valerie Lawson: "Warm, At Last" from *Dog Watch* by Valerie Lawson (Ragged Sky Press, 2007).

Laura LeHew: "Showing Thong" first appeared in the *Elysian Fields Quarterly*, *24*, (2007).

Diane Lockward: "Eve's Red Dress" from *Eve's Red Dress* by Diane Lockward (Wind Publications, 2003).

Christina Lovin: "Girl in a Red Hat" first appeared in *Poet Lore*, *122* (Fall/Winter 2007).

Bobbi Lurie: "January Sales" from *The Book I Never Read* by Bobbi Lurie (CustomWords, 2003).

Amy MacLennan: "Lures" is forthcoming in *Pearl*, *41* (Fall 2009).

Alda Merini: "The Apron" from *Love Lessons: Selected Poems of Alda Merini,* translated by Susan Stewart (Princeton University Press, 2009).

Paul Muldoon: "The Treaty" from *Horse Latitudes* by Paul Muldoon, © 2006 by Paul Muldoon. Reprinted by permission of Farrar, Straus and Giroux, LLC.

Charlotte Nekola: "Trapeze Song" from *New Letters* (Winter/Spring 1986) and *Big Wednesday* (Summer 1990).

Wanda Praisner: "The Hofburg Imperial Palace, Vienna" first appeared in *Circumference, 2* (1993).

James Richardson: "The Family of Ties" from *Reservations* by James Richardson (Princeton University Press, 1977).

Penelope Scambly Schott: "Washing Moon" from *Cool Women Poems,* Volume Two, by Eloise Bruce et al. (Cool Women Press, 2002); © Cool Women 2002.

Lynne Shapiro: "Your Dead Mother" was published in *Myslexia, 36* (January/Feb/March 2008).

Charles Simic: "My Shoes" from *Selected Early Poems* by Charles Simic, © 1999 by Charles Simic. Reprinted with the permission of George Braziller, Inc, New York.

J. D. Smith: "Sweater" appeared in *Settling for Beauty* by J. D. Smith (Cherry Grove Collections, 2005).

Mary Langer Thompson: "My First Pink Slip" was published in *Busenhalter* (Winter 2005).

Helen Pruitt Wallace: "Jane Deals with Infidelity" from *The Tampa Review, 23,* (2002) and in *Shimming the Glass House* by Helen Pruitt Wallace © 2008 (Reprinted by permission of the Ashland Poetry Press).

Ann Walters: "Zen and the Art of Knitting Socks" was published in www.adroitlyplacedword.org. (March 2006).

Lesley Wheeler: "Dressing Down, 1962" was published in *Poetry, CXII* (September 2008).

Irene Willis: "The Yellow Shirt" first appeared *The Laurel Review, 27* (Winter 1993), and then in *They Tell Me You Danced* by Irene Willis (University Press of Florida Contemporary Poetry Series, 1995). Reprinted with permission of the University Press of Florida.

Susan Yount: "Socks of Fire" is online at blossombones (January 2009). www.blossombones.com/index.html

Andrena Zawinski: "Dreamboat" appeared in *Her Mark 2006 Calendar* from Woman Made Gallery in Chicago, Illinois. It also appeared online at *Tattoo Highway*, San Francisco, CA.

Kim Addonizio was born in Washington, DC, in 1954. Her books of poetry include *Tell Me* (BOA Editions, 2000); *Jimmy & Rita* (1997); *The Philosopher's Club* (1994); and *Three West Coast Women*, with Laurie Duesing and Dorianne Laux (1987). She is also the author of *In the Box Called Pleasure* (1999), a collection of stories, and, with Dorianne Laux, the co-author of *The Poet's Companion: A Guide to the Pleasures of Writing Poetry* (1997). She co-edited *Dorothy Parker's Elbow: Tattoos on Writers, Writers on Tattoos* (2002) with Cheryl Dumesnil. Among her awards and honors are fellowships from the National Endowment for the Arts, a Pushcart Prize, and a Commonwealth Club Poetry Medal. Addonizio teaches in the MFA program at Goddard College and lives in San Francisco.

Marcia Aldrich teaches in the Department of English at Michigan State University. She is the author of *Girl Rearing*, published by W.W. Norton and selected as a Barnes & Noble Discover New Authors book. She has just completed a follow-up collection titled *The Mother Bed*. She is the senior editor of *Fourth Genre, Explorations in Nonfiction*.

Sherrill Alesiak has worked in advertising and college teaching, but now enjoys the time to write and to take photographs. Her writing has appeared in many publications such as *Alligator Juniper, The MacGuffin, The Princeton Arts Review, Kalliope, The Owen Wister Review,* and *Blueline*.

Celia Lisset Alvarez is a writer and educator from Miami, Florida. Her debut poetry collection, *Shapeshifting* (Spire Press, 2006) was the winner of the 2005 Spire Press Poetry Award, and she has another collection, *The Stones* (Finishing Line Press, 2006). Her poetry has appeared in *Iodine, Tar Wolf Review, The Powhatan Review*, and other journals and anthologies. She also writes fiction and essays.

Margaret Atwood was born in 1939 in Ottawa, Ontario. She is the author of over fifteen books of poetry, including *Eating Fire: Selected Poems, 1965-1995* (1998); *Morning in the Burned House* (1995), *Selected Poems II: Poems Selected and New 1976-1986* (1987); and *Two-Headed Poems* (1978). Among her novels are *The Blind Assassin* (2000), which won the Booker Prize and the Dashiell Hammett Prize; *Alias Grace* (1996); *The Robber Bride* (1993); *The Handmaid's Tale* (1986); *Bodily Harm* (1982); *Lady Oracle* (1976); and *The Edible Woman* (1970). Among her numerous honors and awards are a Guggenheim Fellowship, a Molson Award, the Ida Nudel Humanitarian Award, and a Canada Short Fiction Award. In 1986 *Ms* magazine named her Woman of the Year. She has served as a Writer-in-Residence and a lecturer at many colleges and universities.

Elizabeth H. Barbato was born in New England and for fifteen years has been a resident of New Jersey, where she teaches English to seventh and ninth graders at a small private school. Barbato was recently nominated for a Pushcart Prize, and her chapbook *Elpenor Falls* will be published by Dancing Girl Press in 2009.

Wendy Barker has published four books of poetry. Her fifth, a novel in prose poems, *Nothing Between Us: The Berkeley Years*, is forthcoming in 2009 from Del Sol Press, and a chapbook, *Things of the Weather*, is forthcoming from Pudding House. She has new poems appearing in recent or forthcoming issues of *Georgia Review, Southern Review, Gettysburg Review, Mid-American Review, The Journal*, and *Harpur Palate*. Recipient of NEA and Rockefeller fellowships, she is Poet-in-Residence at the University of Texas at San Antonio.

Janet Barry is a musician and writer living in New Hampshire, where she works as a music director and teacher and runs her own business tuning and restoring pianos. Janet holds a degree in organ performance and recently earned her MFA in poetry. Several of her works have appeared in the publications *Entelechy, November 3rd Club, Aegis,* and *Off the Coast.*

Rachim Baskin teaches massage, and is a graphic and performing artist. He's creating an independent film, *Life Like a River: Hasidic Stories for All.* He's one of those who are glad to have had a religious education, K-BA. He lives in Cliffside Park, New Jersey.

Jan Beatty's poetry has appeared in *Quarterly West, Gulf Coast, Indiana Review,* and *Court Green,* and in several anthologies. She has three books of poetry from University of Pittsburgh Press: *Red Sugar* (2008), *Boneshaker* (2002), and *Mad River* (1995). She is director of the writing program at Carlow University, where she also directs the Madwomen in the Attic writing workshop. She has also taught creative writing at the University of Pittsburgh. Along with Ellen Wadey, Beatty hosts and produces *Prosody*, a weekly radio program featuring the work of national writers. Beatty currently resides in Pittsburgh, Pennsylvania, with her husband, musician Don Hollowood.

Shaindel Beers's poetry, fiction, and creative nonfiction have appeared in numerous journals and anthologies. A collection of her poems, *A Brief History of Time,* is due from Salt Publishing in London (2009). She is currently a professor of English at Blue Mountain Community College in Pendleton, Oregon, in Eastern Oregon's high desert, and also serves as poetry editor of *Contrary,* and as a poetry reviewer for *Bookslut.*

Nadine D. Boulware is a child of older parents. After hearing stories of the Old South, at the age of eight she began to write. She wrote poetry to express feelings, and short stories based on TV characters to see if she could give them new life. She worked in the travel field for twenty-six years and has been a legal assistant for the past six years, but writing is her passion. She is working on her memoirs, which are as yet unpublished.

Deirdre Brennan was born in Dublin and brought up in Tipperary. Her collections are *Reilig na mBan Rialta* (Baile Átha Cliath, Coscéim, 1974); *Scothanna Geala* (Coscéim, 1989), which was a Poetry Ireland Choice of the Year; *Thar Cholba na Mara* (Coscéim1993); *Ag Mealladh Réalta* (Coiscéim 2000); *The Hen Party* (Lapwing, 2001); *Beneath Castles of White Sail* (Divas Series, Arlen House 2003); *Swimming With Pelicans/Ag Eitilt Fara Condair* (Arlen House 2007).

Michael R. Brown has four books of poetry: *Falling Wallendas* (Tia Chucha, 1994), *Susquehanna* (Ragged Sky, 2003), *The Man Who Makes Amusement Rides* (Hanover Press, 2003), and *The Confidence Man* (Ragged Sky, 2007). He has performed poetry, taught classes, and lectured in various world venues from the South Side of Chicago to South Korea. He created *Dr. Brown's Traveling Poetry Circus,* a theater production which won "Best Poetry Troupe" at the 2004 Cambridge Poetry Awards. He and his partner Valerie Lawson run a poetry series in Maine and have taken over publication of the poetry journal *Off the Coast.*

Megan Buchanan Cherry's poems have appeared recently in *The Sun* and *make/shift.* Her work has been supported by the Arizona Commission on the Arts. A modern dancer, as well as a singer of traditional Irish *sean-os* (old-style) songs, she currently works as the Executive Director of the Tsunami on the Square performing arts festival in Prescott, Arizona.

Enriqueta Carrington's poetry in Spanish and English has appeared most recently in *Contemporary Sonnet, Umbrella Journal,* and *U.S. 1 Worksheets*; it has been nominated for the Pushcart Prize and has received the *Atlanta Journal's* International Merit Award. Her poetry translations have appeared in *Rattapallax* and *A Gathering of the Tribes*. She is the translator of the anthology *Treasury of Mexican Love Poems* and of the poetry collection *Samandar: Libro de Viajes/Book of Travels* by Lourdes Vázquez. Carrington's stories have been nominated for the Million Writer's Award and short-listed for the Historical Short Fiction Prize. She teaches mathematics at Rutgers University.

Billy Collins was born in New York City in 1941. He is the author of several books of poetry, including *Ballistics* (2008); *She Was Just Seventeen* (2006); *The Trouble with Poetry* (2005); *Nine Horses* (2002); *Sailing Alone Around the Room: New and Selected Poems* (2001); *Picnic, Lightning* (1998); *The Art of Drowning* (1995); *Questions About Angels* (1991); *The Apple That Astonished Paris* (1988); *Video Poems* (1980); and *Pokerface* (1977). In 2001, Collins was named U.S. Poet Laureate. His other honors and awards include fellowships from the New York Foundation for the Arts, the National Endowment for the Arts, and the Guggenheim Foundation.

Carolyn A. Dahl's poems and essays have appeared in *Camas, Sojourn, TimeSlice, Suddenly, Echoes for a New Room,* The Helen Keller Foundation's *Reading Lips, The Weight of Addition Anthology, Women Artists' Datebook,* and are forthcoming in *Copper Nickel* (University of Colorado) and *Beyond Forgetting Anthology* (Kent State University). She was a finalist award-winner in the PEN Texas nonfiction competition, has received grants from the Texas Commission for the Arts, been awarded residencies to Hedgebrook and the Vermont Studio Center, and is the author of two books, *Natural Impressions* (Watson-Guptill) and *Transforming Fabric* (Krause).

Elizabeth (Mimi) Danson was born in India, spent her early childhood in China, and ultimately was educated in England. During her adult (United States) life, Danson has taught language skills to children, worked in publishing, and administered an arts center. Her writing has been featured in *U.S. 1 Worksheets, The New Review, Fourth Genre, Anon One,* and other publications. Her first collection of poetry, *The Luxury of Obstacles,* came out in 2006.

Diane Elayne Dees is a writer and psychotherapist in Louisiana. Her poetry has been widely published, and she has also published short stories, essays, and creative nonfiction. A long-time blogger, Diane currently publishes the women's professional tennis blog, "Women Who Serve."

Madeline DeFrees, author of eight poetry collections and two memoirs of convent life, lives and writes in Seattle. Her most recent honor is the Maxine Cushing Gray award from the University of Washington.

Stephan Delbos is a New England-born poet living in Prague, where he teaches, edits the *Prague Revue* and moderates the Prague Poetry Workshop. His work has been featured most recently in *Dirty Napkin, Alehouse, Bordercrossing Berlin,* and *Prague Tales*.

Juditha Dowd's poetry has appeared in journals and anthologies, including *The Florida Review, Passager, California Quarterly,* and *U.S. 1 Worksheets*. Finishing Line Press published her chapbook, *The Weathermancer,* in 2006. She has been awarded fellowships from the Geraldine R. Dodge Foundation, Virginia Center for the Creative Arts, and Vermont Studio Center. A member of the Cool Women poetry ensemble, she reads regularly in the NY Metro area, as well as Portland, OR. She is currently working on a full-length collection of poetry and revising a novel.

Lynn Emanuel was born in Mt. Kisco, New York, in 1949. She is the author of three books of poetry: *Then, Suddenly—* (University of Pittsburgh Press, 1999), which was awarded the Eric Matthieu King Award from The Academy of American Poets; *The Dig* (1992), which was selected by Gerald Stern for the National Poetry Series; and *Hotel Fiesta* (1984). Her work has been featured in the *Pushcart Prize Anthology* and *Best American Poetry* numerous times and is included in *The Oxford Book of American Poetry*. She has received two fellowships from the National Endowment for the Arts and is currently a professor of English at the University of Pittsburgh.

Elaine Equi was born in Oak Park, Illinois and grew up in the Chicago area. She currently teaches creative writing in the Master of Fine Arts programs at City College of New York and The New School. Widely published, her poems have appeared in *The New Yorker*, *American Poetry Review*, and numerous volumes of *The Best American Poetry*. In April 2007 Coffee House Press published *Ripple Effect: New and Selected Poems*. Also in 2007 she edited a special section for *Jacket Magazine*: "The Holiday Album: Greeting Card Poems for All Occasions."

John Estes is the author of two chapbooks: *Swerve* won a 2008 National Chapbook Fellowship from the Poetry Society of America, and *Breakfast with Blake at the Laocoön* is available from Finishing Line Press.

John L. Falk was born in Canada and educated in Toronto and Montreal before coming to the USA and pursuing a career in behavioral pharmacology. Aside from numerous scientific articles and chapters, he is the author of two books of poetry, *Snow and Other Guises* and *Holding Out*, both published by Guernica Editions (Toronto). He has also contributed poetry to many literary journals, including *Osiris International*, *Visions International*, *Prism*, and *The Antigonish Review*. Retired from Rutgers University in 2001 as Professor Emeritus, he is just finishing up a book of poetry entitled *From Quiver to Notch*.

Roberta Feins was born in New York and has lived in North Carolina. She currently works as a computer consultant in Seattle. She received her MFA in poetry from New England College in 2007. Roberta has been published in *Tea Party*, *Floating Bridge Review*, and *The Lyric*. Poems are forthcoming in *Bridges* and *kaleidowhirl*. She is an editor of the e-zine *Switched on Gutenberg* (www.switchedongutenberg.org/).

Linda Annas Ferguson is the author of four collections of poetry. Her newest book is *Bird Missing from One Shoulder* (WordTech Editions, 2007). She was the 2005 Poetry Fellow for the South Carolina Arts Commission and served as the 2003-04 Poet-in-Residence for the Gibbes Museum of Art in Charleston, S.C. A recipient of the Poetry Fellowship of the South Carolina Academy of Authors, she is a member of the Academy's Board of Governors. She was a featured poet for the Library of Congress Poetry at Noon series. Her work is archived by Furman University Special Collections in the James B. Duke Library.

Ellen Foos is the founder and publisher of Ragged Sky Press and a production editor at Princeton University Press. Her first collection of poetry, *Little Knitted Sister*, came out in 2006. A MacDowell Colony and Vermont Studio Center fellow, and a member of U.S. 1 Poets' Cooperative, her poems have also appeared in *U.S. 1 Worksheets*, *Kelsey Review*, *Edison Literary Review*, and *Sensations Magazine*.

Alice Friman's new collection, *Vinculum*, is forthcoming from Louisiana State University Press. Her last book, *The Book of the Rotten Daughter* is from BkMk Press, 2006. She is also the author of *Zoo*, University of Arkansas Press and winner of the Ezra Pound Poetry Award from Truman State University. New work appears in *Southern Review, Georgia Review, Shenandoah, Prairie Schooner,* and others. She lives in Milledgeville, Georgia, where she is Poet-in-Residence at Georgia College & State University.

Christine Gelineau is the author of *Remorseless Loyalty* (Ashland Poetry Press, 2006), winner of the Richard Snyder Memorial Prize, and two chapbooks from FootHills Publishing, *North American Song Line* (2001) and *In the Greenwood World* (2006), as well as *French Connections: A Gathering of Franco-American Poets,* edited with Jack B. Bedell (2007). Her work has appeared in *Prairie Schooner, Connecticut Review, The Iron Horse Review, Green Mountains Review, Georgia Review,* and *American Literary Review.* Gelineau teaches at Binghamton University and also in the low-residency graduate writing program at Wilkes University.

Wally Glickman has been involved with theater (acting, directing, and writing), and has been inspired, especially under the Bush administration, to write poetry. He lives in Rockland County with his wife Eleanor, and has two kids who now live in Seattle and Manhattan. His day job is teaching physics at Long Island University.

Jorie Graham was born in New York City in 1950, the daughter of a journalist and a sculptor. She was raised in Italy and educated in French schools. She studied philosophy at the Sorbonne in Paris before attending New York University as an undergraduate, where she studied filmmaking. She received an MFA in poetry from the University of Iowa. Graham is the author of numerous collections of poetry, most recently *Sea Change* (Ecco, 2008), *Never* (2002), *Swarm* (2000), and *The Dream of the Unified Field: Selected Poems 1974-1994,* which won the 1996 Pulitzer Prize for Poetry.

Susan Grimm is a native of Cleveland, Ohio. Her poems have appeared in *West Branch, Poetry East, Rattapallax, The Journal,* and other publications. In 1996 she was awarded an Individual Artists Fellowship from the Ohio Arts Council. Her chapbook, *Almost Home,* was published by the Cleveland State University Poetry Center in 1997. Her book of poems, *Lake Erie Blue,* was published by BkMk Press in 2004. She edited *Ordering the Storm: How to Put Together a Book of Poems,* which was published by Cleveland State University Poetry Center in 2006.

Carol Guess is the author of five books, most recently the prose poetry collection *Tinderbox Lawn* (Rose Metal Press, 2008). She lives with her spouse, writer Elizabeth Colen, in Bellingham, Washington.

Gregory Hagan holds degrees from the Universities of Iowa and Alabama (Birmingham) and an MA and MFA from Murray State University. His poetry has appeared in *Pudding Magazine: The International Journal of Applied Poetry,* the *Redneck Review of Literature,* the *Journal of Kentucky Studies,* and *Trellis.* He has won awards through the Green River Writers and the Helen Schaible Sonnet Contest. Hagan's poetry reviews have appeared in *Another Chicago Magazine* and the *New Madrid.* He teaches English composition and film at Madisonville Community College in Kentucky.

Rasma Haidri is an American writer living on the arctic coast of Norway. Her work has appeared in many journals, including *Prairie Schooner, Nimrod, Fine Madness, Kalliope* and *Fourth Genre,* as well as anthologies from publishers such as Seal Press, Pudding House, Grayson, Chicago Review Press, Bayeux Fine Arts, and others. Her work most recently appears in *Poem, Revised* (Marion Street Press).

Daniel A. Harris's first collection of poems, *Loose Parlance,* appeared in 2008. He has published some of his poetry in *The California Review, Midstream, U.S. 1 Worksheets, Kerem, Blue Unicorn, Living Text, Evansville Review, Regarding Arts and Letters, Higginsville Reader, Prelaton, Love's*

Chance, Blueline, Silt Reader, Tiger's Eye, and *Poetica.* He has written books on William Butler Yeats, Gerard Manley Hopkins, and Alfred Tennyson, and extended essays on the Anglo-Jewish poets Grace Aguilar and Isaac Rosenberg. He founded JEWISH VOICES: 200 YEARS OF POETRY IN ENGLISH, his education program of presentations and short courses for Jewish organizations (www. jewishvoices.org).

Ishmael von Heidrick-Barnes is a Southern California poet who studied religious studies and theology at the University of San Diego and Surgical Technology at Glendale College. His work has appeared in the *Magee Park Anthology, Tidepools,* the *California Journal* and various other literary publications. He has worked with several well-known poets, including Dr. Sam Hamod and the late Linda Brown. He resides in Rancho Bernardo, California.

Carlos Hernández Peña grew up in Mexico and has lived in various U.S. cities over the past twenty years. His first collection of poetry, *Moonmilk & Other Poems,* came out in 2006. He writes prose in his mother tongue and is currently at work on a collection of short stories in Spanish, yet Hernández Peña crafts poetry in what he terms "this alien language." Recent examples have been published in *U.S. 1 Worksheets* and *Sensations Magazine.*

Beatrice M. Hogg is a freelance writer who lives in Sacramento, CA. She has a MFA in Creative Writing from Antioch University Los Angeles. She facilitates a writing workshop at a local women's homeless shelter. Beatrice is working on several essay collections and a novel. Her essays have appeared in five anthologies and numerous magazines.

Jean Hollander's first book of poems, *Crushed into Honey* (Saturday Press), won the Eileen W. Barnes Award. Her second collection, *Moondog,* was a winner in the QRL Poetry Book Series. Her third book of poems, *Organs and Blood,* appeared in 2008. She has published hundreds of poems in many literary journals and her verse translation of Dante's *Commedia* (with Robert Hollander) was published by Doubleday. She has taught literature and writing at Princeton University, Brooklyn College, Columbia University, and The College of New Jersey, where she was director of the Writers' Conference for twenty-three years.

Janis Butler Holm has served as Associate Editor for *Wide Angle,* the film journal. Her essays, stories, poems, and performance pieces have appeared in small-press, national, and international magazines. *Jonesing for Samantha,* a one-act play, was produced at Manhattan Theatre Source in 2008.

Eric Howard is an editor and poet who lives in Los Angeles, where he knew a costumer named Lori Sacks.

Winifred Hughes is a writer and editor living in Princeton, NJ. Her poems have appeared in *Poetry, Poetry Northwest, Dalhousie Review, Larcom Review,* and *The Literary Review,* among other journals. New work is currently out in *Silk Road* and forthcoming in *Isotope.* A long-time member of U.S. 1 Poets' Cooperative, she was the recipient of a 2007 Individual Artist Fellowship from the New Jersey State Council on the Arts.

M. J. Iuppa lives on a small farm near the shores of Lake Ontario. Some poems have appeared in *frogpond, Brussel Sprouts, Cicada, Haiku Headlines, Amelia* and *Hay(na)ku Anthology.*

Vasiliki Katsarou is a first-generation Greek-American poet and translator of French and Modern Greek. She is a graduate of Harvard College and holds an MFA from Boston University. She has worked in film, and written and directed an award-winning 35mm film called *Fruitlands 1843*. Her poems have appeared in *U.S. 1 Worksheets* and *wicked alice*.

James Keane resides in northern New Jersey with his wife and son and a menagerie of merry pets. He has made his living in magazine publishing, public relations, and advertising for the past 25 years. He has been privileged to have his poems appear in *The Tipton Poetry Journal, Half Drunk Muse, Lily, Plum Ruby Review, Mississippi Crow, Southern Ocean Review, Autumn Leaves, Taj Mahal Review, The Houston Literary Review*, the print anthologies *Harvests of the New Millennium* and *Freckles to Wrinkles*, and *Contemporary American Voices*, where he was the Featured Poet in the August 2007 issue.

Shelley Spence Kiernan lives in Princeton Junction, New Jersey, with her husband and four children. She has an MFA in writing from Vermont College of Fine Arts. Her work has appeared in *Feminist Studies* and is forthcoming in *Ars Interpres*.

Jane Knechtel has been studying poetry writing since 2001, with local and nationally recognized poets, including C.K. Williams, Jack Gilbert, Hugh Seidman, and Nick Flynn. Her work has recently appeared or is forthcoming in *Compass Rose, Harpur Palate, The Mom Egg, A Capella Zoo* and the anthology *White Ink: Poems on Mothers and Motherhood*. In 2006 she was awarded the Parnell Prize in Poetry.

Maxine Kumin was born in Philadelphia in 1925. She has published eleven books of poetry, including *Connecting the Dots* (W. W. Norton, 1996); *Looking for Luck* (1992), which received the Poets' Prize; *Nurture* (1989); *The Long Approach* (1986); *Our Ground Time Here Will Be Brief: New and Selected Poems* (1982); *House, Bridge, Fountain, Gate* (1975); and *Up Country: Poems of New England* (1972), for which she received the Pulitzer Prize. She is also the author of a memoir, *Inside the Halo and Beyond: The Anatomy of a Recovery* (2000); four novels; a collection of short stories; more than twenty children's books; and four books of essays, most recently *Always Beginning: Essays on a Life in Poetry* (Copper Canyon, 2000). She lives in New Hampshire.

Valerie Lawson lives in downeast Maine. She and Michael Brown edit the literary magazine *Off the Coast*. She co-hosted the Boston Poetry Slam at the Cantab Lounge in Cambridge, Massachusetts. Lawson's work has been published in literary journals, anthologies, and e-zines, and her first collection of poems, *Dog Watch*, was published in 2007. She has been nominated for a Pushcart Prize and has won awards for Spoken Word and Best Narrative Poem at the Cambridge Poetry Awards.

Daniel W.K. Lee is a New York City-based poet whose work has been in various online and print publications. He received his MFA in creative writing at the New School and hopes to fulfill his dream of becoming an expatriated cultural juggernaut in the near future.

Laura LeHew is an award-winning poet whose poems have appeared or are forthcoming in such journals as *Alehouse Press, Arabesques Review* (Contemporary Women Writers issue), *Her Mark Calendar '07 & '09, J Journal, Pank, PMS*, and *Untamed Ink*. Her chapbook *Beauty* is due out in 2009 from Altered Crow Press. She received her MFA in writing from the California College of The Arts. Laura received a writing residency from Soapstone and interned for *CALYX Journal*.

Howard Lieberman was originally in the healing arts (a surgeon), but gave them up for poetic ones and, while writing, taught several semesters at West Caldwell College. Now he devotes himself full time to writing and building his web-site, artpoetry.com, which is replete with poems, with accompanying pictures, and history, and a glossary. He has been published in several journals and in the *New York Times*.

Betty Lies is a poet in the schools for the New Jersey State Council on the Arts, as well as a Geraldine R. Dodge poet. Among her four books of prose are *The Poet's Pen*, crafted for creative writing teachers, and *Earth's Daughters: Stories of Women in Classical Mythology*. Lies' new collection of poetry, *The Blue Laws*, was published in 2008.

Lorraine Henrie Lins is currently at work on a book entitled, *I Called It Swimming*, a collection exploring the fear and triumph of family and life challenges. She is two-time finalist for the Bucks County Poet Laureate and a recipient of the Penland Prize for Poetry. Her work has appeared in numerous publications, among them *The Bucks County Writer, The Schuylkill Valley Journal,* and the forthcoming *Mudfish 16*. She resides in Bucks County, Pennsylvania.

Diane Lockward's second collection, *What Feeds Us* (Wind Publications), received the 2006 Quentin R. Howard Poetry Prize. Her poems appear in Garrison Keillor's *Good Poems for Hard Times*, and in such journals as *Harvard Review, Spoon River Poetry Review,* and *Prairie Schooner*. Her poems have also been featured on *Poetry Daily, Verse Daily,* and *Writer's Almanac*. A former high school English teacher, Diane now works as a poet in the schools.

Christina Lovin is the author of *What We Burned for Warmth* and *Little Fires*. A Pushcart nominee and award-winning poet, her writing has been widely published and anthologized. She was awarded the Emerging Poet Award from The Southern Women Writers' Conference and the AWP WC&C Poetry Scholarship. Lovin has been a resident fellow at Virginia Center for the Creative Arts, Vermont Studio Center, and Footpaths House in the Azores. Her work has been generously supported by the Kentucky Foundation for Women and the Kentucky Arts Council.

Bobbi Lurie's third poetry collection, *Grief Suite*, is forthcoming from CustomWords. Her other poetry collections are *The Book I Never Read* and *Letter from the Lawn*. Her work has appeared in numerous print and online journals including *New American Writing, American Poetry Review, Otoliths* and *diode*.

Amy MacLennan's work has been published or is forthcoming in *River Styx, Hayden's Ferry Review, Pearl, Folio, Cimarron Review, Linebreak* and *Rattle*. She was awarded a 2005 Devils Tower National Monument Writer's Residency. Amy currently serves as the program committee chair for Poetry Center San Jose.

Eileen Malone lives in the coastal fog of the San Francisco Bay Area where (after many years of teaching) she reads and writes poetry every day. Over 500 of her poems have been published in literary journals and anthologies, and two of them were recently nominated for Pushcart prizes.

Alda Merini is one of Italy's most important living poets. She has won many of the major national literary prizes and has twice been nominated for the Nobel Prize—by the French Academy in 1996 and by Italian PEN in 2001. In *Love Lessons* (Princeton University Press, 2009), the distinguished American poet **Susan Stewart** brings us the largest and most comprehensive selection of Merini's poetry to appear in English. After beginning her career at the center of Italian Modernist circles when she was a teenager, Merini went silent in her twenties, spending much of the next two decades in mental hospitals, only to reemerge in the 1970s to a full renewal of her gifts.

Susan Meyers, of Summerville, SC, is the author of *Keep and Give Away*, which received the SC Poetry Book Prize, the Southern Independent Booksellers Alliance (SIBA) Book Award for Poetry, and the Brockman-Campbell Book Award. Her chapbook *Lessons in Leaving* won the Persephone Press Book Award.

Paul Muldoon was born in 1951 in County Armagh, Northern Ireland. Since 1987 he has lived in the United States, where he is now Howard G. B. Clark '21 Professor at Princeton University. In 2007 he was appointed Poetry Editor of *The New Yorker*. Muldoon's main collections of poetry are *New Weather* (1973), *Mules* (1977), *Why Brownlee Left* (1980), *Quoof* (1983), *Meeting the British* (1987), *Madoc: A Mystery* (1990), *The Annals of Chile* (1994), *Hay* (1998), *Poems 1968-1998* (2001) and *Moy Sand and Gravel* (2002), for which he won the 2003 Pulitzer Prize. His tenth collection, *Horse Latitudes*, appeared in the fall of 2006.

Charlotte Nekola is the author of *Dream House: A Memoir* (Graywolf, 1995), a work of creative nonfiction, and co-editor of *Writing Red: An Anthology of American Women Writers, 1930-1940* (Feminist Press, 1987). Her writing also includes travel articles, personal essays, poetry and scholarly essays, appearing in publications such as the *New York Times, New Letters, Massachusetts Review,* and *Wide Angle Magazine*. She is a two-time recipient of Fulbright Senior Scholarships in Rome, Italy and Liege, Belgium. She teaches creative writing and American literature at William Paterson University.

Ruth O'Toole earned her MA in English at New York University. She is the author of *Otsu and Other Poems* (Bronze by Gold Press, 2008): a collection of poems inspired by Miyamoto Musashi's *Book of Five Rings*. Her novel *clarissa@loveless.com*, a 21st-century variation of Samuel Richardson's *Clarissa*, was serialized in 2001 by classicnovels.com, and is now available at www.clarissa.loveless.com. She is working on a novel about the rivalry between sex and art.

Carl Palmer, a 2008 nominee for the Pushcart Prize, is the author of *Telling Stories, Memory Moments,* and *Family Matters*, books of flash fiction and poetry performed at open mikes in the Puget Sound region of the Pacific Northwest.

Andrea Potos is the author of two poetry collections, *Yaya's Cloth* (Iris Books) and *The Perfect Day* (Parallel Press). Her poems appear widely in journals and anthologies, most recently in *Women. Period.* (Spinsters Ink), *Beloved on the Earth* (Holy Cow! Press), and *Hunger and Thirst* (CityWorks Press). She lives in Madison, Wisconsin with her husband and daughter.

Wanda S. Praisner is the recipient of a 1995-96 Poetry Fellowship from the New Jersey State Council on the Arts, and fellowships from the Geraldine R. Dodge Foundation to the Provincetown Fine Arts Work Center and the Virginia Center for the Creative Arts. She won the *Devil's Millhopper* Kudzu Prize, the *Maryland Poetry Review* Egan Award, and First Prize in Poetry at the College of New Jersey Writers' Conference. *A Fine and Bitter Snow* was published in 2003 by Palanquin Press (USCA), and *On the Bittersweet Avenues of Pomona* won the Spire Press 2005 Chapbook Competition.

James Richardson is a professor of English and Creative Writing at Princeton University. His books include *Thomas Hardy: The Poetry of Necessity, Vanishing Lives: Style and Self in Tennyson, Rossetti, Swinburne and Yeats* and several volumes of poetry and aphorisms, including *Interglacial: New and Selected Poems and Aphorisms*, which was a finalist for the 2004 National Book Critics Circle Award, and *Vectors: Aphorisms and Ten-Second Essays*, He has recent poems and aphorisms in *Best American Poetry, New Yorker, Slate, Yale Review, Paris Review, Science News*, and *Poetry Daily,*

Penelope Scambly Schott is the author of six full-length poetry books. Her most recent lyric collection is *May the Generations Die in the Right Order*. Her most recent narrative poem is a verse biography of Anne Hutchinson, *A is for Anne: Mistress Hutchinson Disturbs the Commonwealth*. She lives in Portland, Oregon where she writes, paints, hikes, and spoils her family and her dog.

Lynne Shapiro is a writer and teacher who lives with her husband and son in Hoboken, New Jersey. She loves birds and ferns, hats and earrings, surrealists and minimalists. She's had poems and essays published recently in *Myslexia, Trespass, Terrain.org,* and *Umbrella*.

Rochelle Jewel Shapiro's novel, *Miriam the Medium* (Simon & Schuster, 2004) was nominated for the Harold U. Ribelow Award. She has published essays in *NYT (Lives), Newsweek (My Turn),* and in many anthologies such as *What was Lost* (Plume, 2007). Her poetry and short stories have appeared in *Iowa Review, Negative Capability, Coe Review, Pennsylvania English, Stand,* and in many anthologies such as *Father* (Pocket Books, 2000). She teaches Writing the Personal Essay at UCLA extension and reviews fiction and nonfiction for *PW* and *Kirkus*.

Shoshauna Shy's poetry has been included in anthologies by Marion Street Press, Random House, Midmarch Arts Press, Grayson Books, and others. She is the author of four collections of poetry and the most recent one, titled *What the Postcard Didn't Say,* won an Outstanding Achievement Poetry Award from the Wisconsin Library Association.

Charles Simic was born on May 9, 1938, in Belgrade, Yugoslavia. In 1954 he emigrated with his mother and brother to join his father in the United States. He has published more than sixty books, twenty titles of his own poetry among them, including *That Little Something* (Harcourt, 2008), *My Noiseless Entourage* (2005); *Selected Poems: 1963-2003* (2004); *The Voice at 3:00 AM: Selected Late and New Poems* (2003); and *The World Doesn't End: Prose Poems* (1990), for which he received the Pulitzer Prize for Poetry. Simic was chosen to receive the Academy Fellowship in 1998, and elected a Chancellor of The Academy of American Poets in 2000. He is Emeritus Professor of the University of New Hampshire, where he has taught since 1973.

Erin Elizabeth Smith is the author of the book *The Fear of Being Found* (Three Candles Press, 2008) and is currently a PhD candidate at the Center for Writers at the University of Southern Mississippi. Her poetry and nonfiction has previously appeared or is forthcoming in *The Florida Review, Third Coast, Crab Orchard, Natural Bridge, West Branch, The Pinch, Rhino,* and *Willow Springs* among others. She is also the managing editor of *Stirring* and the *Best of the Net* anthology.

J. D. Smith has published two collections of poetry, *The Hypothetical Landscape* (Quarterly Review of Literature Poetry Series, 1999) and *Settling for Beauty* (Cherry Grove Collections, 2005). In 2007 he was awarded a Fellowship in Poetry from the National Endowment for the Arts, and his first children's book, *The Best Mariachi in the World/El Mejor Mariachi del Mundo,* was published in bilingual Spanish and English editions in 2008. He lives in Washington, DC, where he works as a writer and editor.

Elizabeth Anne Socolow, a native of New York City, has taught in many venues, most recently at Rutgers University. A founding member of U.S. 1 Poets' Cooperative, she won the Barnard Poetry Prize in 1987 for her first book, *Laughing at Gravity: Conversations with Isaac Newton.* Her most recent collection of poetry, *Between Silence & Praise,* came out in 2006. She has edited *U.S. 1 Work-*

sheets and is poetry editor of the *Newsletter of the Society for Literature, Science and the Arts.* Socolow's poems have appeared in numerous publications, including *Ploughshares, Nimrod,* and *Ms.* Magazine.

Jill Stein has published work in *U.S. 1 Worksheets, Poetry Northwest, West Branch, MacGuffin, Pearl,* and *Sojourner,* among others. She has received several New Jersey State Council on the Arts grants. She is a psychotherapist and lives in Princeton, New Jersey with her family.

Harvey Steinberg returned to both creative and expository writing after years spent as a labor union jack-of-all-trades, urban affairs executive, environmentalist, and professor of management, law, and labor relations. Since then his poetry has been published in *Wisconsin Review, Diner* (MA), *River Oak Review, Epicenter, Aries, Chaffin Journal,* and in two dozen other literary journals. Also a visual artist, his keenest pleasure is to fuse his photography and painting with his poetry to make seamless works of the two.

Susan Stewart is the author of five books of poems, including, most recently, *Red Rover* and *Columbarium,* which won the 2003 National Book Critics Circle Award. Her many prose works include *Poetry and the Fate of the Senses,* which won both the Christian Gauss and Truman Capote prizes for literary criticism, and *The Open Studio: Essays on Art and Aesthetics.* She is a former MacArthur fellow, a current Chancellor of the Academy of American Poets, and a member of the American Academy of Arts and Sciences.

Maxine Susman, of Highland Park, NJ, is published in many journals and anthologies, including *Paterson Literary Review, Journal of New Jersey Poets, Edison Literary Review, Exit 13, Ekphrasis, Earth's Daughters, U.S. 1 Worksheets,* and *Home Planet News.* She has twice won citations from the Allen Ginsberg Poetry Contest. *Gogama* (Sheltering Pines, 2006) tells of her father, a young doctor in remote Northern Ontario during the Depression. *Wartime Address* (Pudding House, 2008) is the true story of a British woman caught in occupied France. A member of U.S. 1 Poets' Cooperative, she has taught at Rutgers, Seton Hall, and Duksung Women's University in Seoul, and is Professor of English at Caldwell College.

Australian-born **Katrin Talbot** has a BA from Reed College and an MS from UW-Madison. *St.Cecilia's Daze,* her first collection, is forthcoming from Parallel Press. Her poetry and photographs will appear in the upcoming anthologies *Empty Shoes: On the Hungry and the Homeless* (Popcorn Press) and *Cold Shoulders, Evil Eyes* (Wising Up Press). Her poetry has appeared in *Free Verse, Anew Magazine,* many *Wisconsin Poet's Calendars,* in the *Epidemic Peace Imagery Project,* and in several photography exhibits, including *Symphony in Black and White,* and *Visions of America,* a multi-media classical music show and exhibit.

Maria Terrone has two poetry collections, *A Secret Room in Fall* (Ashland Poetry Press, 2006) and *The Bodies We Were Loaned* (The Word Works, 2002). A chapbook, *American Gothic, Take 2* (Finishing Line Press) is forthcoming. Her work has appeared in magazines including *Poetry, Atlanta Review,* and *Poetry International,* and in more than ten anthologies. In 2005, she was profiled in an Iranian literary supplement. Terrone is assistant vice-president for communications at Queens College, CUNY.

Mary Langer Thompson has won poetry and essay awards. Currently an educator in the high desert of California, her articles and poetry have appeared online and in various journals, most recently California Lutheran University's multicultural journal, *The Word.* She lives in Apple Valley, California. Poetry keeps her balanced and sane.

Anca Vlasopolos was born in Bucharest, Rumania and is a professor of English and comparative literature at Wayne State University in Detroit, Michigan. She has published a detective novel, a memoir, various short stories, over 200 poems, the poetry collection *Penguins in a Warming World*, and the non-fiction novel *The New Bedford Samurai*.

Donna Vorreyer lives in the Chicago area and spends her days trying to teach middle-schoolers that words matter. Her poems have appeared in many print and online journals including *New York Quarterly*, *After Hours*, *DMQ Review*, *Byline*, *Boxcar Poetry Review*, *Literary Mama*, *Flashquake*, and *The Hiss Quarterly*. She tries not to take herself too seriously. Visit her writing life on the web at www. djvorreyer.googlepages.com.

Lynn Wagner has poems in *Shenandoah*, *subtropics*, *Rhino*, and *5AM*. She has been awarded fellowships to the Virginia Center of the Creative Arts by the Vira I. Heinz Foundation. Wagner received an MFA from the University of Pittsburgh, where she was awarded the Academy of American Poets prize. A newcomer to Colorado, she maintains a web presence at www.lynnwagner.pbwiki.com/.

Helen Pruitt Wallace's first book of poems, *Shimming the Glass House*, won the 2007 Richard Snyder Poetry Prize and was published in 2008 by Ashland Poetry Press. Individual poems have appeared in *The Literary Review*, *The Midwest Quarterly*, *Nimrod International*, *Tampa Review*, and other journals. She is assistant professor of creative writing at Eckerd College in St. Petersburg, Florida.

Ann Walters lives in the Pacific Northwest with her husband and two daughters. Her poems have appeared in *Poet Lore*, *Poetry International*, *Cider Press Review*, *Fifth Wednesday Journal*, and *The Pedestal Magazine*, among others. She is a Pushcart Prize nominee.

Andy Wass completed the creative writing concentration in 2005, within the University of Maryland's English undergraduate program, as well as the campus' creative writing living-learning program, the Jimenez-Porter Writers' House. In 2004 and 2005 she placed as an Honorable Mention in the Jimenez-Porter Prize for Undergraduate Writing. In 2008 she was a semi-finalist in *The Binnacle*'s Ultra-Short Competition. His poetry has appeared in *The Iguana Review*, *Poetry Midwest*, and *Stylus*. She works as a freelance fashion writer and editor, and is also a musician and artist.

Arlene Weiner has worked as college instructor, cardiology technician, research associate in educational software, and editor. She grew up in Inwood, near Manhattan's northern tip, and has lived in Massachusetts, California, Princeton, and Pittsburgh. Her first collection of poetry, *Escape Velocity*, came out in 2006. A MacDowell fellow, her poems have appeared in *The Louisville Review*; *Pleiades, a Journal of New Writing*; *Poet Lore*; *U.S. 1 Weekly*; and *U.S. 1 Worksheets*.

Lesley Wheeler is the author of *Heathen* (C & R Press), *Voicing American Poetry* (Cornell University Press), and other books. She co-edited *Letters to the World*, an anthology of poems from members of the Women's Poetry Listserv (Red Hen), with Moira Richards and Rosemary Starace. Her poems appear in *Poetry*, *AGNI*, *Prairie Schooner*, and other journals, and she teaches at Washington and Lee University in Virginia.

Irene Willis's poems have appeared in many literary journals, magazines and anthologies, including *Crazyhorse*, *Florida Review*, *Karamu*, *Literary Review*, *New York Quarterly*, *Ploughshares*, and *Women's Review of Books*. She has two collections, *They Tell Me You Danced* (University Press of Florida, 1995) and *At the Fortune Cafe* (Snake Nation Press), which was awarded the 2005 Violet Reed Haas Poetry Prize. Willis lives in the Berkshires in Western Massachusetts, where she works as an educational consultant and as poetry editor for an online publication, *International Psychoanalysis*.

Laura Madeline Wiseman is working on a dissertation at the University of Nebraska, Lincoln. Her creative writing has appeared or is forthcoming in *Blackbird, Grasslands Review,* and *Sonora Review.* Her work has been nominated for a Pushcart Prize. She reads and writes book reviews for *Prairie Schooner.*

Anne Harding Woodworth is the author of three books of poetry and two chapbooks. Her most recent book is *Spare Parts: A Novella in Verse* (Turning Point, 2008). Her essays and poetry have appeared in U.S. and Canadian journals, such as *TriQuarterly, Painted Bride Quarterly, Connecticut Review, Antigonish Review,* and *Poet Lore,* as well as at several sites on line. She has an MFA in poetry from Fairleigh Dickinson University and is a member of the Poetry Board at the Folger Shakespeare Library.

Susan Yount was raised on a farm in southern Indiana where she learned to drive a tractor, harvest crops, feed chickens, and hug her beloved goat, Cinnamon. She is editor and publisher of *Arsenic Lobster Poetry Journal* and works at the Associated Press. She pursues her MFA in poetry at Columbia College in Chicago.

Andrena Zawinski, Features Editor at PoetryMagazine.com, lives and teaches writing in Oakland, CA. Her collections include *Traveling in Reflected Light* (Pig Iron Press), *Greatest Hits 1991-2001* (Pudding House Publications), and *Taking the Road Where It Leads* (Poets Corner Press). Zawinski's work appears widely online and in print. www.poetrymagazine.com/zawinski

Claire Zoghb, winner of the 2008 Dogwood Poetry Competition, has had poems in *Connecticut Review, CALYX, Saranac Review, Mizna: Prose, Poetry and Art Exploring Arab America, Quercus Review, Natural Bridge* and *Through a Child's Eyes* (an anthology on children and war). A graphic artist and book designer on the Connecticut shoreline, she received honors in the 2007 and 2008 Rita Dove Poetry Award and two Pushcart nominations for her work.

Printed in the United States
212011BV00002B/2/P

9 781933 974064